The Perfect Migrant

How to Achieve a Successful Life in Diaspora

Compiled and Edited by

Amina Chitembo

Founder of Diverse Cultures Publishing

Published by Diverse Cultures Publishing, UK

Layout: Amina Chitembo and the Diverse Cultures Squad.

Cover Graphics: Ahsan Chuhadry

Paperback ISBN: 978-0-9957396-9-7

Title: The Perfect Migrant

DEDICATIONS

We dedicate **'The Perfect Migrant'** to all the beautiful souls who have had their hopes for a better life smashed. And those who lost their dignity in a world that looks down upon the brave sufferers, the victorious perfect migrants that made it and now add tremendous value to their chosen destination, where they have settled and made their new home.

We honour and pay homage to all the migrants who have perished ubiquitously around the world trying to escape turmoil, war, or just with hope of a better and mentally healthier lives.

We thank all the people who have accepted us, made our migrant life bearable and supported us through our journeys.

CONTENTS

INTRODUCTION

By Amina Chitembo
Diverse Cultures Publishing

"Every migrant is imperfectly perfect. The strength that drives leaving all you have to pursue the unknown gives you tremendous mental toughness."

The Perfect Migrant book is an anthology that brings together exciting stories from people from different backgrounds who have migrated from their countries of birth to seek a different life in another country. The perfect life that we all yearn for when we decide to move, whether by choice or not, is often fulfilled trying moments, near death experiences and so forth. But what binds the 'The Perfect Migrant' is that life is far from perfect. Nonetheless, the passion, perseverance, determination and sheer strength have seen these authors build the lives that they desire. They have jumped over obstacles, suffered loss and pain, but in the end, they have conquered the elements and made a living in their chosen destination.

"Together we are stronger, our voices louder, and the synergy of our actions more powerful. Together we can prevail on the Navy to put common sense safeguards in place, like requiring its ships to avoid the most sensitive marine mammal habitats and to stop their training exercises during peak migrations."
—Pierce Brosnan

I introduce this book with my own story of migration. My life as a migrant starts way before my final move to the United Kingdom.

I was born in Zambia, from a Malawian father and a Congolese and Zambian mother. This existence pretty much meant I did not entirely belong. I enjoyed my life growing up.

I remember when I was getting married to my first husband, "yes, I am on husband number two, and I have four daughters, two from each." One of his uncles quizzed him. "Where is she from?" he could not answer the question entirely. One of the uncles, who was 'very casual' with me, I will call him Chunga took it up himself to quiz me directly about my origins.

The conversation when something like this:

Chunga: So where are you from?
Me: From Lusaka (Zambia).

Chunga: No, I mean where are you and your people from?

Me: (naively responding, besides I was only 18 years of age and pregnant with no life experience) "Oh my father is from Malawi, and my mother is from Zambia though my grandmother is from Congo."

Chunga: Ati shani? With a frowning expression on his face (what?) Ulimutundu? (Literal translations mean you 'you are a tribe' but in meaning based on the context means you not from our tribe, or you are a foreigner). His facial expression suddenly changed from nice to somewhat serious.

I looked at him, gripped with fear. I could not say anything because I wondered what next was going to come out of his mouth. Right, that moment he walked away from me without any other word. They then had a family meeting where it was decided that the marriage could not go ahead as I was tribeless which to them meant I have no culture, manners or any good qualities that could keep their 'son' in a good marriage.

That was my first real experience of life as a migrant. Well, we went ahead and married their son and made sure I lived a happy life not following any of their traditions. The fact that I was a tribal native did not affect our home. Though, I ended up filing for divorce after 16 years for other reasons.

At the age of 28, I became a migrant again when I moved from Zambia to the United Kingdom. The promise of a good life was not in my mind when I made a move. What prompted the move was to further my education. I wanted to get an education as an Information Technology technician and move back to Zambia after two years. Circumstances changed while in the UK. My family and I decided to apply to remain in the United Kingdom and bring up our family in Europe, for better schools and general lifestyle for the two children and maybe for our own needs too.

The journey has been an experience, trials, tribulations. Successes and failures have been all part of my life. I have failed and succeeded in many ways. I have always been a business minded person. So I have successfully used my power as a migrant to help fellow migrants, by founding and running a non-profit organisation which helped integrated black and minority ethnic communities into the UK life, while working with mainstream organisations to improve policies and make them more inclusive. I did this for ten years. Ultimately, I have been a perfect migrant with a happily imperfect life!

Life as a migrant can be a blessing that you do not see when you are going through a difficult time. It is a lot about mindset. You have to work harder in certain circumstances to integrate yourself without losing who you are. All the influential authors have done that. They have made tremendous contributions and built positive and successful lives where they are in the world.

It is an honour for me as an African woman from Zambia who now lives and runs businesses in the United Kingdom, to present to you this exceptional book. It is filled with remarkable stories of courage and determination.

I am excited to say this book has ten other exciting stories and lessons. I have enjoyed reading and compiling these fantastic stories. I have learned a lot, and anyone who picks up this book will learn a great deal too.

You will read personal and authentic stories from women like;

Angelinah Boniface, who from a village in Botswana moved to the United Kingdom and then, Switzerland. She now works for the United Nations in the United States of America.

Dr. Gianluca Zanini, an Italian whose dream took him from Italy to the Gambia. He shares his journey in pursuit of his desire to become a doctor in Africa. His story is very intriguing.

These and all the other intriguing stories in this book will leave you wanting to read more.

The Perfect Migrant book is a collection of stories of triumph over struggle. The authors share their journeys from their respective countries and finally to settle in a different country and what they have made out of their new life. The richness of the power in the stories will keep you hooked to the end.

It aims to show that there is no such a thing as one size fits all in the life of a migrant. The perfect migrant makes a home despite going through an unexpected turn of events.

WHY THIS BOOK AND WHY NOW
"The Perfect Migrant"

Migrants are almost always seen as burdens to native communities. The picture that is painted of migrants especially in the media has been a grim one, to say the least. Governments are always complaining about; how services are at breaking point and some attribute this problem to migrants who come to take 'services' that belong to the 'locally born' people. It is no secret that some presidents go to any length to build walls and electric wire fences around their border. No day goes by that you hear negative stories about migration and migrants.

Extremist Terrorism has pushed the talk about migration into a debate that people do not want to have.

I invite you to think of the last time you needed medical attention, book yourself into your favourite Italian or Indian restaurant, travelled on a bus or even watched the news. I bet the thought that the person that served you could be a migrant did not even cross your mind. Most of the services in places such as the health services and even educational institutions are provided by people who moved from their countries to make a home elsewhere. Day to day they are just professionals getting on with making people as comfortable as possible.

Well, the truth is they are migrants. Being educated or being in a high position job does not strip away the migrant label. Some of those people fled war, poverty, and hostility to make a life for themselves.

Let me take you back to the definition of the word migrant. For over ten years, I have experienced what it is to be a migrant as an adult, as a professional working with people who are from an ethnic minority background and reviewed several related documents from organisations and experts. Finding an all-encompassing definition of the term 'Migrant' or 'Immigrant' opened up more questions than answers. I have not seen any that is as clear as the one from the International Organisation for Migration (IOM). Below is the answer to the question;

Who is a migrant?
IOM defines a migrant as any person who is moving or has moved across an international border or within a state away from his/her habitual place of residence, regardless of; (1) the person's legal status; (2) whether the movement is voluntary or involuntary; (3) what the causes of the movement are; or (4) what the length of the stay is.

I like this definition because it is all-encompassing, some experts and indeed governments try only to describe migrants are only illegal migrants.

This book is about reclaiming the term and showing the other side of the life of migrants. It is also about raising awareness of the life of being a migrant and the fact that migrants are people just like natives. We have stories to tell and aspirations.

The Migration Observatory at the University of Oxford, a body that informs debates on international migration and public policy, produced a briefing entitled:

Who Counts as a Migrant? Definitions and their Consequences.
The briefing raised the following four interesting, vital points:

1. Definitions of 'migrant' vary among different data sources, and between datasets and law. Among other possibilities, migrants may be defined as foreign-born, foreign nationals, or people who have moved to the UK for a year or more.
2. Different definitions have significant consequences for data, both regarding numbers of migrants (stocks and flows) and the analysis of the impacts of migration.

3. The use of the term 'migrant' in public debate is extremely loose and often conflates issues of immigration, race/ethnicity, and asylum.
4. Conflicting definitions pose challenges for policy, particularly since many 'migrants' are not subject to immigration control and legislation.

I agree with all of the four points above, and there are a lot more interesting points that I cannot fit in this book.

The 'cheeky' but serious title of the book **"The Perfect Migrant"** from my search for meaning and trying to understand what a perfect migrant life would be like if that existed. I invited people to share their stories to contribute to the book without giving any parameters. The result was an attention-grabbing array of compelling stories.

These experts by experience have poured their lives into this book to show you our reader that despite going through struggles in the foreign land, one finds the strength to keep trying and find time to make a positive contribution to the world. The book is also an opportunity to share what we have learned with the broader society.

You will learn about life as a woman's IVF journey, and a teenage mum who beat the odds to work at the united nations and this is only a selection.

THE RICHNESS OF DIALECTS AND AFRICAN ENGLISH

The authors of this book have all migrated from their home country to live in another country. They come with the richness of writing and speaking in more than one language. These are real stories, and people have used their day to day English, which may seem wrong to some readers. The aim is not to have a polished book but one that introduces you to the life of the author in their language, vocabulary, and richness of the everyday words that they use. If you are looking for 'native English' perfection, you will not find it in this book. We made a conscious decision to ignore the Oxford, Cambridge, Harvard or any other English rule and instead showcase the way we speak in the day to day life. It is my sincere hope that you will enjoy and learn how beautiful the variety of language and sentence formulation is when you are not a so-called native English speaker. Even a person like me who was born in a British Colony and pretty much spoke English from the day I learned how to speak.

The correct English was drummed into me in School, arriving in the UK was a shock because I have moved from South to North and West to East and pronunciations and vocabulary in varied. So, it is totally impossible to know what correct English should be. In addition to that, I grew up speaking Benglish (Bemba a Zambian language is mostly spoken in the northern part of Zambia and the provinces such as Lusaka and the Copperbelt mixed with English in one sentence) and Nyanglish (Nyanja another language/dialect that is mainly spoken in the Eastern Province and Lusaka and English in one sentence).

The composition is fun, and we love it. We hope you will love it too. The authors make no apologies for who they are and have chosen to embrace that in this book.

I thank you, dear reader, for your support by buying and reading this book. I am sure you will find very intriguing and educative.

Please buy some copies for your loved ones too. The proceeds go a long way in spreading the message of the positive contribution of migrants.

Enjoy!

Beatrice Hofmann

Beatrice Hofmann born and raised in Uganda moved to Germany in 1999. After 18 years in her adopted home country, she views Germany as the focal point in her life. With this unique background complimented by extensive global travels, she sees herself as a cosmopolitan. She  enjoys sharing her experiences and the exchange of information with people from all walks of life. Sharing her knowledge and wealth of experiences with other people and helping them foster their personal growth, gives her great joy. Aside from her professional involvement, the author is the mother of a 17-year-old daughter, and together they enjoy venturing out on shopping sprees and visits to other wellness facilities for fun and studies.

Books include: (1) The Perfect Migrant: How to Achieve a Successful Life in Diaspora (2) Leading: How to be your own Boss!

Company/Business Name: Nu Life Professional-Wellness

Area of Expertise: Wellness, Consultation of African Migrants

Training/Speaking /Seminar Topics of interest include (1) "How Long Does One Remain a Migrant" (2) "Upcoming Entrepreneur Award 2015" of the African Women in Europe, Geneva, Switzerland (3) "KITEV" —co-founder of a free university in the city of Oberhausen, Germany

Contact Details:

https://www.facebook.com/beatriceakello

https://www.linkedin.com/in/beatrice-hofmann-44b488110/

Phone: Business: +49 208 46 71 54 93 | Cell.: +49 178 836 29 47

Email: nulife-info@gmx.de | beatricehofmann@gmx.de

Websites: www.massageoberhausen.de

Chapter One

☙

LEARNING EACH STEP OF THE WAY

By Beatrice Hofmann

INTRODUCTION

How to Identify Opportunities and Benefit from Them

Born in mid-1970ies Uganda, I grew up in one of the bustling capitals of Eastern Africa. It was in Kampala that I was prepared for life. Going through my schooling years, spending countless hours with my father and a big brother who taught me so very much about people and the world in general. It was in Uganda where I had my first crush on a fellow student from the neighbourhood and learned the ropes to become the croupier at famed Casino Paradise. Soon I was promoted to the main cashier because my managers appreciated my accuracy and trusted me.

"The first light of human consciousness and the world's first civilisations were in Africa."
—John Henrik Clarke

At the verge of adulthood, I felt content with my life and was ready and eager to explore what it held in store for me. At twenty-one, I travelled to Nairobi, Kenya. It was my first time outside of my homeland, and it opened me up to the idea of seeing other parts of the world and other cultures.

A SIMPLE TWIST OF FATE

It was at that time I met a foreign traveller at the Airport in Nairobi, together with his friend Michael we travelled to the islands of Zanzibar. Wanderlust had brought him to Africa to see the continent and get to know its people. It wasn't before long that our curiosity and a general liking for one another had us both falling in love.

So, when a few months down the line my new-found partner had to leave back to his native country Germany, I was invited to visit him and his country.

> **"The choices we make within the boundaries of the
> twists of fate determines who we are."**
>
> **—John Perkins**

Happily, I asked for some vacation time at the casino, and soon I was on my way to see more of the world I had only known so far through school, books, TV or movies. Off I went for what was supposed to be a three-month visit to experience Germany and its people. Towards the ending of the second month, my partner and I found out that I was pregnant. The doctor said it could be life-threatening to make the air travel back to Uganda and so the decision was made for me to stay for the time being.

To make my stay easier on the legal side, my partner and I decided to get married. It was not a decision that came easily to me. Back then, occasionally, I felt like being trapped, since the original idea was to come on a vacation and see and experience something new. It was never my intention or plan to stay and settle into family life; not that early on in my life.

Instead, I found myself increasingly isolated and realising what life-altering changes a child and marriage would mean for me personally as well as for my family back home in Uganda. The situation I had slid into rather naively went against any standards my own family had ever taught me to live by.

DIFFERENT CULTURES AND EXPECTATIONS

Living in Germany soon proved somewhat overwhelming for me. It was a completely different culture, with different infrastructure and a language I did not speak at that time. All of this put me in a state of shock. The only person I knew to some extent was my partner and newly-wed husband, and with time I began to get to know his family. Before he went on to work, he would first drop me with his parents all through the pregnancy.

After work at 7 pm, he would come home to pick me, and we would go back together to the place where we lived in Wesel-Friedrichsfeld.

A small city, with a suburban to the somewhat rural environment, nestled between one of the centres of Germany's most industrialised regions, the Rhein-Ruhr-Area and the Dutch border.

In May 1999 I had come to Germany; three months later in August I got married and found myself adapting to my new last name of Hofmann. It took me a long time to tell my dad about my situation. At first, I confided in my big sister, who told our mother. For me, my father was a person of the highest esteem, and since I knew he would have a tough time understanding the situation I put myself in, I could only muster up the courage to inform him as one of the last ones in my family.

When he heard my story, naturally, he was distraught, since for him, a marriage and having children is understood as part of a process and not something done in the rush of a moment out of wedlock. Only a full six months later, the day my daughter Sina was born, and he was informed about the event, and that his choice for the middle name "Atim" (meaning: the first child born away from home) was used, he made peace with the situation.

AN IMPORTANT MEETING

Seven months into my pregnancy I met Mike from Uganda at a bus stop in my new German hometown of Wesel. We struck up a friendship, and he showed me how to use trains and told me where to take German lessons. My new friend was very kind and helpful in teaching me what he had seen and learned in and about Germany.

"Learn the language—the gateway to the culture."

He pitched and emphasised the idea of me learning German time and time again. In fact, he asked me to do him a favour to learn the language, because he perceived it as the gateway to the culture and stressed that it would be of immense help to me to become an integrated and an active part of the German community.

His well thought through advice have had an immeasurable impact on my life as much back then as to this very day. I'm very grateful to him and miss our regular meetings as he moved to England some years ago to raise his own family.

HAVING A DAUGHTER AND GETTING A WHOLE NEW FAMILY

For Sina's birth, my oldest sister came to visit for one month and helped with the household chores, which is a tradition in Uganda. She arrived right after labour since Sina came two weeks before her due date. During the time of her stay, my sister realised the dynamics within the family and commented to me that Sina's grandparents seemed quite dominating. An observation that stayed with me, but whose impact would only reveal itself to me in the ensuing months and years.

Soon after Sina was born my husband and I moved with our baby daughter into the house of my in-laws. It was during the following year that I increasingly realised that I found myself only on the sidelines of the on-goings in my new family. The parents-in-law took centre stage from buying things (stroller, food, etc.) for Sina to taking care of her.

The only thing that my husband and I got to buy for Sina back then was a pair of socks that I took a liking to. However, with no money and a restricted ability to communicate I felt much of the time powerless, and like my life, as well as the one of my husband and our daughter, had been hijacked by my in-laws. Without any responsibilities and no opportunity to work, I saw no role for myself in this family scenario.

Throughout my three years within the family, I got to cook exceptionally rarely. My husband usually turned to ask his mother to find out about our daughter's state of being or discuss whatever the topic of the day was. The family did not actively try to engage me and help me to integrate into the new environment.

Instead, I spent my days mainly confined to the house and my in-laws and husband, and only very rarely introduced me to their friends or acquaintances. The only trips our whole family unit conducted together throughout my life with them was one to the little town of Norddeich on German's North Sea coastal region and one to Füssen in Southern Germany (Allgäu region) while I was still pregnant with Sina.

Whenever I was heading with my daughter Sina to take a stroll to the local playgrounds, I was met with a close observation of my German family. Usually, there would be a call coming in from my mother-in-law each hour or hour and a half as she wanted to know our whereabouts and what we were doing.

The call was often answered to by other German mothers whom I met at the playground since my mother-in-law did not speak English and my German was still limited at the time. The situation turned more and more into a very suffocating experience for me.

FIRST ATTEMPTS AT ASSIMILATION

When I approached my husband and parents-in-law with the idea that I wanted to learn German and take lessons, the thought was met with some resistance. It was communicated to me that I did not need to learn the language. Upon my insistence, I was enrolled in German lessons at the local Volkshochschule and very soon began to go there regularly once a week.

> **"Leadership is about doing the right thing, even if it is going against a vast number of naysayers and mediocre people."**
> **—N. R. Narayana Murthy**

Nonetheless, I started feeling increasingly isolated. I witnessed how my husband's brother, who was married to a Thai woman who'd been in Germany already for seven years, had arranged his family life. His Thai spouse remained untrained in the German language and kept very close to the family with not much outside contact. And so, I began to worry that I was going to be for much of my life similarly closely controlled by my husband's family.

Since then my former sister-in-law from Thailand had often come to consult me when she was facing any family issues. My advice to her remained consistently the same.: If you believe, you need your car, and any other material belongings then continue to live like this. If you want to give up being other-directed, then you have to make your own choices and face the consequences. Nowadays, my ex-sister-in-law runs her massage salon in Switzerland and calls me her mentor, which brings a smile to my face whenever she says it. She feels content with her life, and this is what is most important.

After spending one full year learning German at the local Volkshochschule (VHS—a German adult learning institution sponsored by the local communities to help its residents to further their education free of cost, or at least at very reasonable prices in a variety of different areas of knowledge), and have only gone through 32 pages of an accompanying textbook, I had turned very frustrated with the little progress I had made.

WITH PERSISTENCE AND A LITTLE HELP
FROM MY FRIENDS

I was wondering if there were a better way of progressing at a much faster pace, and so I consulted another male friend from Uganda. Simon was studying at the university in Heidelberg. He advised me to take German classes at a university. When I approached my husband about this, his reaction was that it was too expensive. It would cost more than EUR 150 per semester. Finally, I found out about a summer intensive German course at the University of Duisburg-Essen and insisted that I wanted and needed to go. Finally, my spouse obliged.

At the school, I was told that, if I wanted to learn German free of charge I needed to enroll into the university and get into the German program language for University Entrance (Deutsche Sprache für den Hochschulzugang - DHS). Since I had completed my high school diploma successfully in Uganda, I was eligible for enrolment and followed through with official matriculation, which was supposed to be followed by my concentrated studies for German language, literature, and history.

In April 2001 I commenced with courses running five days a week from 8 a.m. to 12.30 p.m. and doing my homework after that. My German family realised at that time, during the conversation with friends, that none of them had gone to university to study, but I was now immersed in such.

> **"Without continual growth and progress, such words as improvement, achievement, and success have no meaning."**
> **—Benjamin Franklin.**

Suddenly the family was seeing an issue with me being out of the home until the afternoon hours and not helping with one-year-old Sina as much as they thought I should. Shortly before the course ended my husband created an argument. Telling me that, I was sitting around doing nothing instead of getting a job. I knew I wasn't ready yet and was hoping to continue my advanced education. I still had a lot of learning to do to have a command of the German language that would allow me to work in an interesting and demanding position, helping me to succeed in an adequate career.

Back in Uganda, I was used to making a good living with my earnings from my work at the casino. All my family members in Uganda always placed high importance on learning and getting a good education and so I felt this was the route I should be taking as well. Anyway, shortly after that, I completed the DHS course.

> **"Live as if you were to die tomorrow. Learn as if you were to live forever."**
> **—Mahatma Gandhi**

My German family continued on a daily basis with mood swings and an often quite a negative outlook towards my very own aspirations and outlook on life. Complaining when I wanted to buy something, or when my mother-in-law bought me clothes or other things that I was supposed to wear despite not being to my taste.

So eventually I approached my husband to tell his mom not to buy me any clothes, shoes or other things anymore. I was used to determining my lifestyle from Uganda and wanted to remain my person overseas. I became disappointed that I had a daughter whom I could not be the mother I wanted to be. The majority of the care-taking part was taken on by my parents-in-law. I had a husband who was to a large extent just the extension of his parents reach and did not make many of his own decisions.

> **"Learning is not attained by chance; it must be sought for with ardour and diligence."**
> **—Abigail Adams**

My new German family did all it could to discourage me. I had always enjoyed singing in the choir back home in my youth, so for a short time, I started singing in a band in the nearby town of Dinslaken; we had two live concerts in Dinslakenstadthalle (Townhall) and Jaegerhoft, a famous discotheque in the region. More and more I began to look for new activities to enhance my life experience.

FIRST PROFESSIONAL STEPS IN GERMANY

To prove myself as a provider, I answered to an advertisement looking for a housekeeper for the enterprise Mövenpick in the nearby city of Essen. It was at this job that I met Mary Mirie Njoki, who to this very day I call my closest friend, mentor and greatest inspiration. This position also led me for the first time out of the rural and contemplative little town of Wesel-Voerde into an urban environment in Germany.

My mother-in-law continued to be the homemaker. She cleaned and cooked and took care of Sina. I only did the cooking about five times during my three and half years with the family. Some of this cooking happened over the Christmas visit of Simon and his family, who came to stay for three days but left after just one night.

My impulsive husband's vibe was not the one pouring out hospitality. He looked down on my friends and me. So, Simon and his family decided to leave early despite initially having different plans. I felt embarrassed, realising that I even couldn't have friends over, because of the food being smelly. The reasons were embedded deeper than this. I was asking myself, how could I build up something, when I was facing a hostile scenario every time.

Next thing, my husband was getting upset with me and started complaining. The reasons were that I occasionally got home 30 to 60 minutes late, since after work I, at times, sat down with my friend Mary to talk. Arguments ensued during which I tried to make my side understood, explaining that I was trying to rebuild my social life and establish new friendships. Eventually, I asked my husband and Mary to sit together to allow each of them to hear a second opinion and gain a better understanding of the overall situation.

> **"Progress lies not in enhancing what is, but in advancing toward what will be."**
> **—Khalil Gibran**

With Mary, I started exploring my surroundings in Germany. So, one day I received an invitation for the first time to a party in Düsseldorf's Old Town. I encountered a bustling city life which I knew to some extent from my former life in Uganda's capital Kampala. Now working together with Mary and making a little income of 600 Euro per month through my part-time work, I started building up my circle of friends. Over the following months, I began to regain the confidence and the will to carve my niche in this new world. I felt good for the first since I had come to Germany.

SEPARATION AND DIVORCE

At home though arguments ensued much more frequently. Usually, I was being accused of not looking after my child anymore. One day, coming home from work? I found a letter from a lawyer, accusing me of coming home late and abandoning my role as a mother. With the help of Mary and Britta, I consulted a lawyer to come up with a response.

> **"It is not a lack of love, but a lack of friendship
> that makes unhappy marriages."**
> **—Friedrich Nietzsche**

My lawyer said that my chances of receiving child custody, in general, were quite good; only that for to gain physical custody, I needed to have a personal place to live. I was forced to give up the confines of my family life for the pursuit of a more hopeful and positive future, which I wanted to find on my own together with my daughter Sina. So, I went on the hunt for an apartment nearby.

Soon I had to find out that, whenever I called, or latest showed up in person, I would not be ending up getting the apartment. Then another letter from my husband's lawyer arrived, stating that my work conflicted with me being a fitful caretaker for Sina. At the recommendation of my lawyer, I quit my job with Mövenpick.

In the meantime, my husband followed up with his legal pursuit of the custody of Sina. He went to court and claimed that I was unfit as a legal custodian without any own shelter nor a job to provide for Sina. He even laughed at me for taking so long to find an apartment. The court went ahead and granted him custody under the given situation only to reconsider in the case that my position would have changed for the better.

Having been forced into a situation with no job and continuously upsetting efforts made in finding my adequate accommodation for a living, I finally thought up a ploy. I let a German friend come with me to consider an apartment I had taken a liking to. It was affordable, at a good location and perfectly met my needs?

Together we went with an assurance letter from Sozialamt (Germany's Department of Children and Families and Social Welfare Office) to the landlord. Fortunately, I had already made savings of 1.200 Euro from my work at Mövenpick in my bank account. So, I could take over the kitchen built into the apartment and buy the needed basic furniture.

Finally, the apartment was given to me after a period of drought and a desperate search for five months. When I showed my husband the contract to rent the apartment, he broke down in tears and realised that it was no longer a laughing matter. At this point, with a new apartment within walking distance just 1.7 km away from my in-law's house and sufficient financial support waiting for the move. I seemed to be well equipped for a future life together with my daughter living in my apartment.

In the midst of this situation, I met a German friend at the weekly market in my hometown and told her about the latest developments and that I had just received another letter from the courts. My friend suggested having a closer look at the latest communication between the lawyers and the court. Then I discovered that the very same day was the due date for me to file a complaint against the latest verdict. So, I put in my complaint just in time to have the courts reconvene for another session.

During the next court date, I was finally attributed with having the accommodation and means to provide adequate care for Sina, and as a result, I was granted physical custody to the dismay of my husband and his family. In fact, the judge was pleased with me trying my best to assimilate within the German society by having made successful efforts to learn the German language, enrolling into university and taking on a job on my own.

> **"The secret to happiness is freedom . . . And the secret to freedom is courage."**
>
> **—Thucydides**

After many discussions with my closest friend Mary and giving it a thorough thought myself, I concluded to let Sina remain with my husband's family in the same family unit and physical environment she had gotten used to during the first three years of her life. With me as her primary caretaker as a working single mother would have meant hardship for Sina for many hours during each work week.

Me just living a 20 minutes foot walk away from my daughter's home, would allow me to be always within reach when needed and to see my daughter on a regular basis. I have always kept in mind that, whenever Sina wanted to come to see or even live with me, I was ready to welcome her with open arms. I saw and continue to see this for my daughter Sina as the most conducive environment to experience an even-handed and well-adjusted life under the given circumstances. In 2004, one year after this final ruling regarding child custody, I became officially divorced from my spouse.

REBUILDING MY LIFE

With the legal situation in between my ex-husband's family and myself resolved and the living situation established, I began to focus on rebuilding my life in my chosen new home country of Germany.

My primary focus was on my personal development. I then enrolled in as many courses at the local Volkshochschule as I could, and at the same time looked for a more demanding job that matches my career aspirations. It proved to be a very long journey.

"Education is the key to unlock the golden door of freedom."
—George Washington Carver

For three and a half years I received rejection letters after rejection letters on all jobs of interest which I applied for. Meanwhile, I was working in low-level jobs and taking care of Sina as much as possible.

Through all these years emotional or other support from my very own African family was lacking. My relationship with them was always met with demands for financial support, which I could not meet. After my divorce, I was told that I had brought shame to the clan. Nobody in my family had ever gone through a separation. I was the only one. Today I am glad that this happened. It was an eye-opener for me. Nobody in my family should ever stay unhappily married again.

The social welfare department was eager to put me into a program for Health and Care (Gesundheit & Pflege). The program consisted of half a year theoretical training and half a year hands-on experience in the workforce for Caritas. Making 1 Euro per hour, but getting further training over the coming year, so I went for it.

By accident, I found a school specialised in cosmetics in a close by city. I felt inspired after trying for so long to find a job in which I could apply my brains without success. I decided to dedicate my manual labour to contribute to my community and carve out my niche in Germany's professional world. The school gave me an education in cosmetics against a tuition fee of 4.640 Euro for my vocational training.

During that period I saw an ad in the newspaper from the German Job Centre (a division of the government-run unemployment office), which was offering job placements through vouchers that would be going to various employers.

"Innocence is thought charming because it offers
delightful possibilities for exploitation."
—Mason Cooley

So, I started working for Burger King with the help of such vouchers, which were introduced to put people to work through placement incentives for the employers. To the dismay of many people, such vouchers were quite often misused by employers to cash in on employees hired only for the shortest possible period. After getting the subsidies paid out in two installments after the first six weeks of employment and then after six months of hiring somebody, too often employees were let go and very soon after the next one was hired.

Eventually, even the German government realised the misuse and ended the program in 2012. Unfortunately, I fell victim to this scheme and my time with Burger King came abruptly to an end. Nonetheless, I was able to cover the school tuition for the cosmetics school with my earned money along with some funds coming from another friend from Germany who gave me a significant loan.

STARTING MY CAREER IN WELLNESS

On completion of the cosmetics program, I began applying for relevant positions. The first best option presented to me came in the form of an internship that was offered by the wellness/spa department of the Nikko Hotel in downtown Düsseldorf for four months. The Nikko is one of the exclusive Molton Brown spas in the world. Molton Brown is well known for its cosmetics based on natural raw materials, for which I have undergone special training. During the first week of my time at Nikko, I wasn't allowed to do anything though, because the management still lacked faith in me.

Then I finally got a chance with one customer, who was very satisfied with my work. And the very same day seven more customers would follow, all voicing their praise. Eventually, I was approached for a full-time position; however, at this point, I had already agreed to a full-time job offer at a cosmetics shop in Leverkusen.

"By appreciation, we make excellence in others our own property."
—Voltaire

At Bel Etage cosmetics, at that time the biggest parlour in Germany, I was working with the meagre pay of 700 Euro gross income. Nonetheless, I had given my word and felt committed, though it meant even more of a commute and less money; instead of 50 kilometres each way, I now continued to travel 75 kilometres.

My new assignment in Leverkusen's beauty parlour gave me a lot of satisfaction as I was quickly taken on a vast variety of duties covering everything from performing all procedures offered to clients as well as administrative and managerial jobs to fill in for my manager. However, I noticed repeated verbal threats from my manager to the staff, which were completely and consistently directed at foreign women. In addition to that, my working and commuting hours were becoming longer and longer, with the pay barely covered my living expenses. Therefore, I decided after three months to go back to the Nikko Hotel in Düsseldorf and take on their standing job offer.

Over the next two years, I worked for Nikko. The workload was extensive, long weeks with lots of overtime; nevertheless, despite the hard work, I learned a lot about cosmetics as well as wellness concepts and their application.

Eventually, I was burnt out and needed to take some time off to recoup. At times I felt desperate, I wasn't sure if I wanted to continue in Germany. My relationship with my daughter Sina required fixing. My ex-husband and his family had instilled the idea in her that I had planned to take her away and bring her to Uganda with me when she was small. A friend was ready to help me settle in the USA, and I knew I had to find something that would fill up my life with joy and happiness. Discussing my thoughts with Sina, it became clear to both of us that, my place was near her. Our discussion back then in 2009, not only helped mend my relationship to Sina but turned out to be as well the beginning of a new idea which increasingly floated the corners of my mind: Work independently, stop being other-directed.

After a few months, I continued my work as a beautician and massage therapist at cosmetic institute Rita Ott, just a few kilometres from my own home. I immensely enjoyed the work but saw that many of the ideas I brought to the table were either not implemented, or the benefit was only reaped by the lady owner of the business; thus, the idea of opening up my enterprise started to grow within me.

Aside from my regular job, I started attending additional seminars and workshops to further my knowledge in various massage techniques. So, I started to gather ideas to finally put down my very own concept of a unique wellness enterprise. My idea was to offer a combination of a broad variety of wellness techniques within the frame of an African spiritual environment to allow for the utmost soothing and resuscitating experience for my clients.

> **"There are no secrets to success. It is the result of preparation, hard work, and learning from failure."**
> **—Colin Powell**

REALIZING MY DREAM OF A "NU-LIFE"

With the business plan I had written up, I went to the German Arbeitsamt (Unemployment Agency) and applied for a loan of 5.000 Euro to cover for the down payment of the first two months' rent and the basic equipment I still needed to purchase. These were to help me to survive for at least the first three months during which I hoped to gain a considerable customer base. Unfortunately, despite turning in all required documents to the authorities, the loan was not granted.

A request for a micro-credit through a local bank was also refused because I had no security collaterals. Finally, I was able to start up my business with the financial help of several of my friends.

A very generous friend was willing and able to do what no bank or government institution was ready to do, and so I still received 5.000 Euro. My very own sole personal investment was my meagre savings of 420 Euro from my tax returns of the two previous years, which invested in my first promotional efforts of flyers. My sister

Cathy, who moved to Germany a few years after me, paid for my first rent.

It certainly turned out for the better that way, because I would not have been in the position to repay the loan to the authorities within a half year period as it was stipulated in the contract. In fact, the 5.000 Euro loan I received from my friend was eventually dropped and thus given as a generous gift and a proof that true friendship works without strings attached. I've come to see it as a sign that honest and genuine behaviour will be rewarded. In fact, all the loans that were given to me, I received without any contract or securities. It might seem unbelievable, but it is true.

> **"Your positive action combined with positive thinking results in success."**
> —**Shiv Khera**

It would have been virtually impossible for the first two years. Taking a very long slow road helped me to set up my enterprise for the success it has become. All of this because my concept is a unique one and my clients first need to get used to the environment and appreciate the whole experience. For this to sink into my target audience in and around Oberhausen and the surrounding Ruhr Valley area did not happen overnight. In the summer of 2018 my business, Nu-Life Professional Wellness, celebrates its eighth anniversary and is finally well established in the community. As Michelle Obama said in one of her speeches; when you have worked hard and done well and walk through the doorway of opportunity, you don't slam it shut behind you. No, you reach back and give other folks the same chances that helped you succeed.

My customers come from all walks of life; from the city council, business owners to blue-collar workers and students. It makes me proud to see what has developed over time, especially that all my toils and the hardships I have gone through, since coming to Germany, have helped me to draw many good conclusions that have pointed me into the right direction toward a better future.

GIVING BACK TO THE COMMUNITY

I have come to the realisation and understanding that without the help of other people, I would not have been in the position that I am in today and thus embrace and wholeheartedly enjoy when I can lend a helping hand and give back to the community.

Over the last five years, I have been involved in a variety of organisations and projects, which at heart always hold the core idea of helping society progress to a brighter future with an emphasis on helping to integrate people and their ideas into the community.

We all know that what is important to us is family, friends, giving back to your community and finding meaning in life.

Since 2011, I am an active member of the PETEK network, which is a German group consisting of female entrepreneurs all of whom are migrants. The goals of this organisation are to be the voice of migrant entrepreneurs in Germany. The group is actively advocating and lobbying for migrant business people and within its weekly recurring meetings discussing interesting new business, social, and political developments. The group is a very helpful resource for any budding as well as a seasoned entrepreneur.

In 2014 I participated in the Forum D'Avignon together with a small team of people with a concept to raise awareness for the inclusion of migrants within societies in general. Together we developed text and a workshop for schools and interested socially involved groups with the title "How Long Does One Remain a Migrant."

With this program, we wanted to show both sides of the community, migrants and natives alike, which both can benefit from one another. Of course, to realise the full potential to the maximum, it is necessary to work together with an open-mind and heart. Our participation in the Forum D'Avignon won us a nomination for the finals. That same year our Text won us the first prize, "Fair.Rappt" competition of the Jugendhilfe Essen, which was looking for innovative Texts, This resulted in several newspapers approaching us for interviews as well as the BR (Bayerische Rundfunk), producing and televising a segment with us.

In 2015 I started as a member of the socially and artistically involved organisation KITEV the foundation of the "Freie Universität Oberhausen." The goal of this project was to determine the possibilities of a university in the city of Oberhausen, covering all of the requirements from the majors, to the faculty, location scouting to the financing. The project is still ongoing and continues to draw a lot of attention from within the city of Oberhausen and beyond.

Life changes all the time so that we can change the world.

WHAT TO LEARN FROM ME?

I achieved so much with the support I received from my network of friends and acquaintances. Be there for people when they need you, they will return your favour when the time comes. Partake in social functions to build your network. A key factor is to learn to network with the right people. For this one has to understand the difference between good and bad criticism. A good tool for this is using a SWOT analysis (identifying the Strength, Weaknesses, Opportunities, and Threats) of the people in question. Conducting such analysis periodically on my own business as well as family situations has also helped me to sharpen my understanding of my very own position.

Invest in yourself. I have done many seminars; even some political ones through Konrad-Adenauer-Stiftung. Participate in anything that triggers your interest. I have done TV shows just for curiosity's sake. It sure has helped me to gain exposure. Nowadays, it happens that some folks ask me for my autograph in Germany. Never do fear!

"I learned that courage was not the absence of fear, but the triumph over it. The brave man is not he who does not feel afraid, but he who conquers that fear."—Nelson Mandela

After all the tragic setbacks, I can finally say today that, I have found myself as a person. I am usually happy and content and look forward to every day I get to wake up. Funny enough, I've got to give credit to my ex-husband who has been an inspiration to me all along with his words that, I would not be able to manage to live in Germany without his help. The icing on the cake came three months after I had started "Nu-Life" in the form of a letter from the Jugendamt (Department of Children and Families), which asked me to pay child support to my ex-husband since he was demanding for it. It was another attempt to make life difficult; fortunately, this issue got settled over the course of the following year with the help of our teenage daughter Sina. I've never received any such requests again.

I've made my way, because of my pride, confidence and at times stubbornness. The advice I gladly pass on to anybody is to stand in for your convictions and do your own thing—follow your dreams and lend a helping hand wherever you can. Learn to ask for help and give the same to whoever asks for it.

Find people that inspire you, with their ideas or deeds. For me, my friends Mary and Simon, as well as Oprah Winfrey, have been shining their bright lights on my lifetime and time again.

Never forget your roots, but always keep an open mind. And never stop learning, always keep eager for new information. Stay honest, because this builds trust.

DEDICATION

Though it is my very own journey, I could not have done it without the help, support, and encouragement of so many. Some of these angels of mine just touched my life briefly, and in passing, others accompanied me for many years, some of them are still very close to me. I would like to use this opportunity and express my deepest gratitude and appreciation to all of you.

My very special thanks go out to Britta, Cathy, Erwin, Gerrit, Hans-Gerd, Jochen, Lema, Mary, Myka, Pauline, Rhodah, Rose, Shamim, Theresia, Thomas, Thorsten, my daughter Sina and my family, especially my dad—Thank you!

THE FIRST REVIEW BY MY FRIEND RHODAH

"Hi, Bea. You are fiery at all levels. Your autobiography is a clear very personal life journey of yours particularly in the German diaspora. I congratulate you for re-collecting all those steps, pains and struggles of your life. It is good for self-healing."

Charity Ngugi-Latz

Charity is a Kenyan, mother of five young adults who reside in Köln, Germany. She is a graduate of the University of Nairobi. BA (Hons) in Literature 1981. She worked for many years as an insurance underwriter in Kenya. In 2015, she enrolled as a Volunteer in the Sprachraum (Köln library for refugees) and Red Cross.

She is a qualified community reporter, and she is deeply involved in youth community projects in Nairobi Kenya and Afro-Diaspora projects in Germany. Currently, she works as an administrator and researcher for Sonnenblumen Community Development Group e .V, an international NGO in their Köln office

In her own words Charity says:

"My passion for writing migrant stories stems from my first-hand information and the need to give voice to them."

Area of Expertise: (1) Digital Storytelling and Spoken Word. (2) Agent of Dignity

Books: (1) Co-author of 'Across borders for dignity' (2) Co-author of The Perfect Migrant

Speaking and Seminar Topics: (1) Dignity (2) Identity, Recognition, and inclusion

Contact Details

Social Media: @CharityWairimuNgugi-Latz

E-Mail: wakamauson12@gmail.com | cwlatz@yahoo.de

Websites and Blogs

http://www.unmaskedstories.org

http://www.anencounterwithgod.com

Chapter Two

❧

ACROSS BORDERS IN SEARCH OF DIGNITY

By Charity Ngugi-Latz

INTRODUCTION

"We are the fabric of creation . . . interwoven."

My passion for writing on migration and my experience of cultural diversity stems from a deep-rooted, constant, nagging desire to give voice to the millions of migrants on planet earth. This passion was even more awakened by observing and interacting with many immigrants in Germany, listening and watching the news on both the local and international media.

I finally concluded that one of the primary reasons that we people migrate is because we are all in search of some form of a new and worthwhile dignified life. Whether we travel willingly or unwillingly, we leave behind our lives of great value. Yes, we choose to cross borders and reside in unfamiliar territories because we yearn for a different life from what we were born into.

In this chapter, I write from my heart.

I recount my thoughts and tell my story authentically.

My story comes after a self-therapy and an alone-time holiday retreat. During this period, I have taken time to reflect on my life. I have reviewed many experiences within me and many personal discussions with other migrants I have encountered.

Over time, I have had discussions with many migrants of all ages, gender and ethnic backgrounds coming from various countries, such as Syria, Kurdish-Turkey, Iran, Iraq, but, mostly from the African countries, because these were the ones allocated to me by the Red Cross refugee offices and other migratory bureaus where I have worked on voluntary basis three times a week. My main duties have been assisting them with translation, accompanying them to the foreign offices, helping with train connections, food purchases and other essential day to day necessities.

These great opportunities have helped me tremendously, transforming me into a more empathic, mindful person and have increased my concern with the plight of others; those less fortunate, or with more or less similar backgrounds to mine, but find themselves in disadvantaged situations and are unable to express themselves freely.

These encounters have also helped me acquire a lot of insights into the diverse cultures in Europe. They have made me more appreciative of the traditional richness, and yet interestingly they revealed the entangled underlying oneness in humans. We are interwoven as a human race and in our humanity.

My sincere hope is that this chapter will be of great value to you dear reader, and act as an inner lens to some of the migrant's untold," unmasked stories."

I will also give some tips, but not as a professional expert in this field, but as an intuitive immigrant, recounting my personal, living experiences during my almost twenty years in Germany and my keen observations too.

MIGRATION AND MARRIAGE
"Migrating is as Old as Eons"

The migration or exodus of a people from one country to another is a sensitive topic, and that is why I choose to refer to it as; *"The crossing of borders in search of dignity."* Migration is as old as the creation of the world or as eons, old-times in memorial. However, Migration and its connection to all the immigrants has become a ubiquitous, misconstrued word with many negative connotations to those who bear the reference. Hold that thought. I will explain this thought further, later in the chapter. I will explore how this is especially true in Europe and other developed countries.

I am an African woman of Kenyan descent. I was born as the first of three children in April 1959 to an Air Hostess mother and an Arts and Crafts Educator Father.

I migrated to Germany in 1998, where I got married to my German husband Helmut Latz in 1999 until his passing away due to cancer illness in 2014. We lived together in the city of Cologne in a beautiful, quiet, middle-class residential area known as Delbruck. I still live there to date.

Our first year of marriage was peaceful and very exciting for both of us since it gave us both the feeling of a home and the bondage of marriage which we both needed so badly.

My husband was a widower after a 32-year marriage. He was very willing to get married, mainly because as he confided to me, he loved me. He was a homely person, but he had never lived in a home without a mother or wife or cooked a meal for himself all beyond boiling an egg. From my side of the story, 1 had no complaints; he was like manna from heaven.

I had just met a man who loved me and had helped me escape a very traumatic, violent, seventeen-year relationship with the father of my four children in Kenya. My firstborn child was from a previous relationship while at the university and lived with his father. Having met my husband through my cousin during an outing, it was love at first sight. He and 1 talked so much, and I found myself recounting all my life and my plight. He invited me to bring my children to his hotel in the following days, and 1 did, of which after one enjoyable afternoon spent together at the Pan- Afric Hotel, he proposed to me. With some much joy 1 said Yes. The conditions of my life that he saw in Kenya had prompted him to invite me to Germany and ask for my hand in marriage. He accompanied me to the German consulate in Kenya, and there I was granted a visa for three months.

Before agreeing to travel to Germany or to marry him, we had a spoken agreement. We reached a deal that one year after getting married, and settled in Germany, we would arrange for my children, two boys and two girls, aged ten, five, four, and three to join us so that we could live as a family in Germany. He agreed to adopt them or sign for the foster-parenting.

Our wedding, which was held near the Köln-Dom Cathedral at the marriage offices, was very beautiful and we had over 100 guests most of them being from my African community and their partners mainly Germans. Six months after the wedding, I travelled to Kenya where I legally obtained consent from the father of my four children, before a commissioner of oaths. I got approval for their full parental custody and consent for their adoption to Helmut as a foster parent. Their father at the time was also suffering from a chronic illness, and he willingly saw their residency in Germany as a wise decision. (He has since passed on nine years ago to date)

One of the major humiliating circumstances was our living conditions. We were living in a Mud-thatched one-roomed house. It was a very pitiful reality that prompted Helmut and me to agree to get married immediately. God had finally answered my prayers. I saw how this opportunity would give us new beginnings, a new, healthy life as a family.

It was exciting!

I was able to get a work permit, and once I arrived in Germany, I sought immediate employment as a cleaner in a five-star hotel. The work was very, very hard, but l was adamant, and my primary goal was to ensure my children moved to better living quarters, went to better schools and that l could save for their air tickets and other travel expenses to join us in Germany.

I did not want to burden my husband who was 25 years older than me and on pension status, and therefore, and therefore, did overtime hours. At home, I took care of all the house chores. We went out with my husband occasionally and were happy at the beginning. My husband contributed to the rent and other utility payments. We were living pleasantly.

However, things took a dramatic turn for the worse when l returned from my one month visit to Kenya and approached my husband with all the relevant papers so that we could initiate the migratory process for my children. My husband seemed to have consulted with his local pub drinking partners seeking advice and had been fed with some negative information and advice. After a while, he became agitated at the very mention of my children. He was verbally abusive towards me; he started using a lot of racial hatred language in the house. At first, I was very annoyed and even approached his friends at the pubs seeking clarification. I was shocked because some of them I had started considering as close friends and I thought they genuinely liked me as a person as I did them. After three or four confrontations, I felt the isolation and hostility and stopped going there.

During sober moments my husband would consent on going to the offices the next day, but by afternoon or evening, when I returned to him, it was the same long, shouting, abusive drama. He even went so far as to hide the correspondence from the juvenile foreign offices, and after some time he adamantly declared he was not ready to move to 'some migrant infested area.' It was a surprising turn of events for me. I had to find a different way to bring my children to come and live with me. So, I engaged a lawyer to help me with the consent papers for the children and at the Federal office for migration and refugees.

My husband refused to sign them which meant I was unsuccessful. Because of my meagre earnings. My children could not travel to join me in Germany. In the course of some confusion on his side, he had signed one formula for one of my sons, and he was able to travel and arrive at the age of 13 years but only on a three-month visa.

However, after a hard struggle, a three year long, legal battle where I spent all my financial savings to pay the lawyers and court fees something positive came out. As a strong and educated African woman, I was not ready to give up the battle, and at the last judicial hearing where they had given my son two final weeks to leave the country, there was the empathic heart of the old Helmut that came back briefly. After a long talk with a juvenile officer, my husband consented to the adoption of my son. This was one big win, I will never forget.

Many years later we would talk about this moment with my son and I would ask him how he felt those days and at that moment. He said that at that moment he just wanted to get out of that judge's office and scream with joy. How did I feel? L felt numb for some few days; l kept on thinking my husband might go back and re-sign and have a change of heart. But one beautiful episode happened. Three weeks later, l got a form addressed to me on behalf of my son to go to claim six years child allowance owed to us. Because my husband did not cease with the abuses and his refusal to help get to the other children l made a choice. We took the cash and travelled the two of us to Kenya, my son for ten days and l for two months. I built a three bedroom house for my children and eventually moved them there. I banked the rest of the money for my son and at the age of sixteen paid for his (Ausbildung) further education and driving licence.

WHAT MARITAL OR CO-HABITING TIP CAN L GIVE?

My story and that of many migrants are a common occurrence with the same or similar characteristics and consequences. The very idea of marriages of conveniences, or "paper -marriages," happens more often than we want to admit especially with the increasing internet meetups and online dating platforms. There is absolutely nothing wrong with this trend, but it can get seriously dangerous especially where marriage is no longer considered as a sacred, life union.

Children outside these marriages must be seriously taken into consideration before any commitments can be made, preferably signed legally documented agreements. Divorce is also a frequent, disconcerting and tiring experience and more so if you are an immigrant and the process might not be in your favour. As an immigrant, if you have not acquired a permanent residence, the probability, and threat of being deported back home without you being prepared sticks with you.It is a constant shadow and threat pushed down your throat as a reminder every day. The insecurity can even contribute to one being deemed unfit, and because of the emotional toll, one can even lose custody of the children in a marriage gone sour. (has happened to many). Engaging a lawyer for every court appearance or visit is a costly affair. Many illnesses and deaths have occurred in the last twenty years. One can attribute the primary cause to the stress of imbalanced life partnerships.

THE PERFECT MIGRANT SCENARIO

Picture this scenario; I share this from my perspective. It is controversial, and others may disagree, but I want to share it from my point of view based on experience and discussions with people in situations similar to mine. Wanjiru is twenty-four years old and is from Kenya. Her partner George is a divorced, German native. They couldn't be more different; from diverse cultural backgrounds, different upbringing, and different careers. Wanjiru is a Hairdresser and George a Builder-roofing-Mason. The two met on an online dating site, and after three months of long daily chats, there is a high romance. George even proposes marriage on Skype and Wanjiru accepts.

He sends her an invitation and an airline ticket to come to Germany. In her haste, she hardly consults any older adult, and in her ecstatic joy, she accepts, even resigns from her job, gives up her rental-flat, says her joyful goodbyes to family and friends who are more than envious and glad for her too. She arrives in Germany, moves in with George and within two months of her three-month visa, they get married at the attorney general's office. It was a simple wedding of fewer than ten people; only one Kenyan lady is her guest in this simple, no pompous wedding.

What both had not taken into account and had taken for granted is their wild and high expectations of each other. Wanjiru had this magazine-kind of the myth that she would be marrying into this rich, handsome, lavish, high-class hotel and shopping lifestyle to this European, ever-loving, romantic man with no flaws.

George, on the other hand, may have envisioned a different woman. He always had this idea of a wild African tigress in-bed woman from the African continent, docile by nature, naïve and ignorant, one who cannot think for herself, especially on financial matters and willing and always there at his beck and call.

A woman wife-servant to do his house chores, controlled, not to be consulted. An unintelligent woman dependant on him. George has never even visited Africa. His image of the African continent, or its people and its culture is limited to what he sees in the media.

The reality sets In. Wanjiru's dream is shattered, first by the weather, the loneliness, the language barrier and the commanding tone and behaviour of her husband. She no longer accompanies him to the local pub or football games. She has no money, and her husband no longer loves nor ready to discuss anything. She is just another person in the house.

Now given the scenario above what do you think happens next?

Would you run?

Would you call home and say you want to come home?

From observations, hardly does anyone in this dilemma make these decisions. Usually, you stay and hope things will work out well soon.

Of course, soon is never soon enough before other drastic consequences follow. Of course, the shame of being laughed at by your peers, the guilt that you have let your parents down, and the slight inner lies you tell yourself, that your man loves you, hinder you from taking any action. There is also the most significant reason; you don't do anything because you have No idea of how things work in this foreign country and where to run to.

What is the major difference?

Cultural diversity plays a significant role in inter-marriages because of the simple fact that these are two intelligent persons with limited knowledge about the upbringing conditions of the other. However, like in all other relationships even of persons from the same tribe or race, what is important is the foundation of that relationship which ideally should be built on the mother of all languages which is Love.

In my many interactions, I have met many mixed couples. Some are married, and others are not, but living wonderfully and raising healthy stable children.

The top five things I love about mixed marriages are:

1. Three specific marriages between an African and a German come into my mind. The children are raised by one parent speaking the African mother tongue at home and the other parent speaking the German language. The very idea of multiple languages spoken in a single home is a positive skill learned at an early age.

2. In mixed-marriages there is the chance to have a rich and diverse cultural learning, especially when the families visit the different countries, getting to experience the different landscapes, traditions, foods, songs, and sceneries.

3. Where there is harmony among the parents, the children also get to know and appreciate their two or three identities as one, and this helps to erase the possibility of these children growing up without inferiority complexes based on their skin colour, hair texture or other racist attitudes.

4. Subsequently, in any form of relationship of mixed race or not, being sensitive to the very fundamental role of not violating the other person's dignity is paramount.

5. Respect, sharing in the activities and decisions is a respectful approach without being too critical or judgemental listening and learning from each other can produce some very creative ideas especially in the mixture of arts like music, food and mode styles. I have discovered that listening in any connection can help eliminate some of the very expectations at the beginning of any relationships.

My personal experiences from mixed marriages are that I have learned a lot of German songs especially sung during the March/April 5-day festival in Cologne. It is one of the most spectacular, pleasurable, loving periods of the year and a lot of interactions takes place, giving one a chance to meet the native German in a relaxed atmosphere. Summer is also a good time to interact and be in a jovial mood since it is usually less than three months of sunshine.

MY ALCOHOLISM AND PSYCHOLOGICAL PROBLEMS
"Fighting for my children and my dignity."

It all started with the lies, abuse, and broken agreements and they had their toll on me. The background was working against me.

The story of my struggle as a wife and a mother.

My efforts to belong in a foreign country.

My battle to fight for my children and their rights to live with their mother.

My struggle to ensure my son's RIght to be with his mother, and not to be repatriated back to Kenya as if he were an orphan, was not violated

I thought I had no way to escape.

It was very humiliating for us because despite the fact that my son was a minor, and I was his sole legal guardian, married to a German native they still wanted to deport him. *"It is a story not openly spoken about, but one that occurs amongst many migrants lives where law separates families."*

It is

This story will help my reader understand the depths of crossing borders in search of dignity. The whole drama, the broken promises, the separation from my young children at a tender age, it all affected me deeply both psychologically and emotionally. I no longer had the strength, the courage, the self-esteem to engage in any more legal battles.

The language was also a significant hindrance. I encountered a lot of impatience from the government officials since I could not coherently state my case every time I put in a re-file and continually broke down and walked away from the office in tears and broken. This is the reason I engage my free time in voluntary work.

MINDSET CHANGE TO FEND FOR MY CHILDREN
"Children are the anchors that hold a mother to life."
—Sophocles

As a mother, I had to do what I needed to do since I could not bring my other children, to come live with us. Whatever avenues I tried did not work. I am not a woman that gives up, and I almost surrendered. In life, they are many objections and obstacles. How you deal with situations depends very much on your mindset.

There is always a way that you can solve a problem. You must think hard. For me, the fight to bring my children to live with me was too hard. Eventually, I faced the fact that I was losing my head and all my hard-earned cash to the legal system which was not working in my favour. I had to move on but without jeopardising the promise and love of keeping my children safe.

The situation broke my heart, but it did not eradicate me, nor did it drive me to divorce my husband. Instead, I made a point of enrolling my children in Kenya, in boarding schools. I moved them to a new home and employed a full-time house-keeper. I then started visiting them three times a year during their one-month holidays.

I would like to be a bit more vulnerable and tell you something. Although I resolved not to bring my children to Germany, I was miserable, unhappy in my 15 years of marriage. A lot of things were not going right. Somewhere along the line, I lost my confidence and lost my self-worth.

I turned to alcohol, and before I knew it, I was struggling with alcoholism on and off.

I felt in my battles that my migrating decision had been a wrong decision. I felt guilty and neglectful as a mother, and like a second-class, inferior citizen.

I felt ashamed as if I had compromised my social status.

There, I was in Kenya, a graduate of the University of Nairobi, with a Bachelor of Arts, honours degree and a major in literature. For 15 years I had a great career as a life insurance underwriter and training officer in middle-management with big corporations in Kenya. I got myself into a wrong relationship and quit my jobs. Now, here l was again in a foreign land, with an unhappy marriage, doing menial jobs and struggling with alcohol.

DEPRESSIVE MELANCHOLY

I hated my menial jobs; my dreams had been shattered. The alcohol would numb the pain for a while. And within my scope of friends, in very similar situations, we as migrants consulted each other and did not trust or rely on government information. We relied on our togetherness as migrant communities and did relatively help one another and console each other too.

However, now that l am older and wiser and have a broader perspective about the migrant situation, l would like to discuss depression. I can say without an iota of doubt that l was depressed. Although l never sought any medical help, either for my traumatic experiences of domestic verbal abuse, lack of custodial stay with my children and my alcohol problem, l know that l would have been clinically diagnosed as depressed. Most of us were undergoing similar problems, but we resigned ourselves to thinking and accepting this as our destined life. Am l justifying this? No! I am trying to give clarity to this kind of situation and the way we went about dealing with it before, and to some lesser extent, we still deal with it in the same way to date. We ignore the idea of seeking medical attention for emotional issues since these types of situations are termed as insanity or madness especially in our African cultures. We care what people will think or say about us. I could drink for two to three days over the weekend without going home or sleeping. Isn't that sick?

I have known migrants who have done that to date but do not seek medical attention here in Germany although it is free and available. I am not judging anybody, but I believe it is imperative for one to seek healthy alternatives rather than consume excessive alcohol, partake in drug and substance abuse, remain in isolation, live in unhealthy environments or be in an unhealthy relationship and constant denial.

I advise mothers or women undergoing domestic violence in Germany and the world, please seek help. Get out, get counseling, search google for social workers' services or send me a message on my Facebook messenger. The important thing is to seek help because these are problems that cannot be easily solved alone because by nature they are deceptive. One can not see their reality in this situation because of fear. There are several positive aspects of migrants. Immigrants, this includes asylum seekers; in that community groups become a necessity born out of the need to be heard, to belong, to feel included and safe. I will write about this later on in the chapter.

THE POSITIVE OUTCOME OF MIGRATION

"Self-love, care, and finding yourself are the best gifts you can grant yourself."

—Amina Chitembo, Author

Approximately four years ago after the death of my husband I started on a self-therapy.

I went through many phases of committed church-going and participation. I went into a lot of online research on spirituality and seeking to find my purpose, knowing I needed help and stability. One of the significant things that happened is that I just had this great awakening in my heart especially when the news was perpetually flooded with the influx of immigrants and a lot of them dying at seas, deserts and refugee camps to be involved.

I suddenly realised that I was very fortunate in that I was free, a permanent resident in Germany and my children were now grown up with the youngest now over 20 years old.

I decided to play a more active role and voice their plight, and through small concrete steps l did the following:

1. Enrolled for the German language courses at the Volkhoch-Schule (German Language school in Köln).
2. Attained my Germany language B1 (second level) and integration certificates. These are very relevant to enter the job field as they are proof one understands the history and politics of German and the basic language and therefore, one is eligible to do other courses.
3. Enrolled in the Basic Computer courses, Community Reporter courses: in the field of Video (Digital storytelling) and script writing.
4. I created two websites and wrote articles as well as blog. Did a lot of digital storytelling.
5. Research for free online writing and speaking classes. Registered with social activists' websites that have great articles on immigrants, spiritual growth, and personal development.
6. Registered as a volunteer with Refugee organisations like the Sprachraum a library for immigrants with free digital and physical services and integration activities.

These voluntary jobs gave me access to the refugee camps or homes and enabled me to interact with refugees, built on their trust to open up even on personal matters. I went further and together with others we founded the Sonnenblummen Community Development Group (e. V). This is where l am currently working both as a volunteer and part-time worker in their headquarters in Cologne. Its main agenda is to incorporate all the different cultures and express them into the world. It is a highly dynamic movement, the first of its kind in

Germany, and it is an international organisation for the Afro- diaspora community.

All these interactions, self-planned studies have helped me to regain my confidence, and I have now become a positive thinker.

I have also since then been very closely connected to a lot of native Germans, and other persons from other European countries like Spain, The UK and Italy and I now have a broader perspective about all of us.

I make it a point to attend other countries cultural events, and it's incredible how much we have in common, and how much there is to learn about the arts, dance, music, food, languages, dress and hairstyles. There is for example in Cologne, Germany the "Summer Jam" where people, young and old from all races, travel from all over the world to attend this Reggae Festival with its colours and fashion styles that are so fascinating together with the music with a One Love message.

FINAL WORDS AND LESSONS LEARNT
"We are all one, we each have value to give one another."
—Charity Ngungi-Latz, Author.

Things might not turn out how one envisions them to be, before migrating to another country. But on the other hand, staying home if your heart wishes to move on is not an answer. Hope is the key to everything. Many people have made it to the top, or achieve their dreams and live a better life.

The meeting of many minds, the diversity of many cultures mixing and getting entangled through marriage, business partnerships or during social interactions is a good thing. It is progress in action. Through social bonding, we build new co-operations and collaborations. However, we each need to caution ourselves, not to allow any superiority complexes to dwell in us.

We need to appreciate ourselves as co-beings and not competitors or perceiving ourselves as the dominant person. We each have value to give one another. Further education to acquire more skills is also an excellent motivating factor in migrating.

There often is a wrong perception, the classification of the 'migrants' into this one huge, massive box of a people looking for handouts. Or out to destroy the economy of "first-world countries" by taking fewer wages, therefore, rendering the natives jobless. This myth should be done away with especially in a country like Germany where the government regulates the job salary.

Secondly, this is a caution to those migrating for no other reasons but on economic grounds. If one is coming from a no-war zone declared country, then your hard-earned money that one gives to people peddlers or "modern-day slave traders" is lost. Parents who send their children with such savings from maybe sold land and so forth. I sincerely suggest it were better if some of that money was used to secure a start-up business for your child right there in your home country.

Your child will most probably end up in an asylum camp, with a "Duldung"—that is a stamp that does not allow them to work, go to school or even travel from the area they are designated to stay. They are not first or second or nor any citizens, and some have been in such conditions for years waiting for deportation.

Remember:

"East or West, North or South. Home is Best".

When you receive offers for working abroad, research. Go to online forums and ask openly.

Do not keep things a secret, it is how you perpetuate crime and the deaths of many who have died on the journey to "first -world countries." These worlds are not gold mines. The laws have become very stringent for illegal immigrants. Joblessness and poverty are not only limited to Africa, for example.

Africa is becoming an investment hub. And rather than always chasing a University degree acquire other skills like carpentry, plumbing, agricultural and technical knowledge.

In this short space I believe that migrating for reasons other than war, hunger, or other unforeseen circumstances, it is better to adjust to the public environment close to the family.

There is nothing like "free" anything!

Everything comes with a price.

Nothing free comes easily, especially acts done in the dark.

Awareness and transparency are critical.

Laura Tinzoh

Author, Motivational Speaker, Moderator, and Founder of 'LaTinzoh Empowerment.' Her book 'From the Inside Out' and multi-annual conferences and workshops cover themes that are intended to uplift, inspire and foster Spiritual Growth. In her daily Podcast series, Practical Theology, she shares her day-  to-day experiences as a Christian within and outside her family; her struggles and the ultimate triumphs, which come as a result of her faith in God. The series is posted weekdays on Facebook and What-sApp Messenger.

The multi-talented mother of five launched the Women Empowerment Summit in August 2017. This annual event is aimed at challenging women to step out of their comfort zones and do extraordinary things. The first edition of the conference, which took place in the summer of 2017, was attended by many women from across Germany and Europe.

Books include: From the Inside Out (English) Aus dem Inneren heraus (German)

Company Name: LaTinzoh Empowerment

Area of Expertise: Public Speaking, Workshop coordination, Event moderating, Writing, Podcast, Living the Christian Faith every day. Coaching/mentoring, Spiritual Growth, Marriage Enrichment, Women Empowerment

Contact Details:

Social Media: @Laura Tinzoh | @LaTinzoh Empowerment

Telephone No: +41734068799;

Email: forr_ngaba@yahoo.com

Chapter Three

☙

LIT IN THE DARK

By Laura Tinzoh

INTRODUCTION

Twenty years later and I still get the chills each time I remember the feeling in my tummy as the plane started to move. Of course, my dream came true. I landed in Berlin, and there was no one to pick me up. Oh, dear me! There I was crying and shaking as I walked towards the Airport exit in the hope of seeing a black woman there waiting for me.

Now how do I pass through this huge glass door without a handle?

Lord have mercy! I stood in a corner waiting to see if anyone else would succeed in opening a door without handles. Maybe the tears blinded my eyes, and I couldn't see . . . at some point a tall white man walked in from the other side, and the door just opened . . . just like that.

How could that be possible? Yes! Witchcraft! Well, I dashed through the door before it could close . . .

If you have had the great opportunity to move from your home country to the 'developed' world as they say you might relate to this feeling.

Did you experience something similar when you just arrived?

What was going through your mind?

How was your visa process and preparation?

How did you feel the first time you entered a plane?

If on the other hand you are reading and wondering what I am talking about and you have not travelled this perfect or not so perfect journey. I hope you will enjoy reading my story, learn something new from it and get some idea of what life as a migrant can be like.

"NOBODY SAID IT'LL BE EASY"

It was a mixture of feelings. I wasn't sure what to do. Yes, I was excited about going to the *white man's* land, but I wondered how I was going to cope without my family. Without the guidance of my parents and the company of my siblings and friends. I couldn't hold back the tears.

The weeks leading up to the d-day had been hectic. Filled with shopping, drying of Vegetables and other food items (you know, my mum had to make sure I don't starve to death), arrangements with the contact person in Germany, farewells and much more . . . I remember my hands shaking as I stared at the visa in my passport.

The process which I heard was always complicated was a-b-c for me. Just that year, the German Embassy had canceled the condition of passing the language examination at the B2 level. Talk about God's Favour. Unlike other horror stories I had heard, I didn't even have to get in for an interview.

SO, IS THIS REALLY HAPPENING?

Douala, August 26th, 1997: Sitting on this colossal plane all alone made reality very real.

What had I gotten myself into?

Had I just signed my death warrant?

What if something went wrong and the plane crashed immediately after take-off?

I had heard the stories. What if I got to Berlin and there was no one to pick me up?

What if my parents' warning came true and I got pregnant immediately I got there?

What if I couldn't pass the language test and got sent back to Cameroon?

Oh, the questions just kept flooding in . . .

If you are reading this today is proof that the plane didn't crash, right? But sometimes I sure wished it had happened. The first days and weeks in Germany were, let's say 'strange.' There was a little bit of excitement, sadness, and anxiety but above all SHOCK! I grew up knowing that 1 pm meant 4 pm- that's how we rolled. We don't want to talk about teenagers walking half naked and kissing on the street, do we?

Life in Germany sure has been a roller coaster. I have seen it all and experienced it all. There were days when I thought it was over . . .

Like the night I slept under the train station in Holzminden, weeks after my arrival in Germany. It was cold that October night. I still remember the dog sniffling around me, still trying to decide which part of my body would taste best. His drunk master dangling away was in no hurry to check on his companion. I held my breath and my Rosary tight . . . telling God ". . . even if I should die, Father, being eaten by a dog is not a good way . . ."

Have you experienced something like this before?

When were you sure you would die?

What happened?

The good thing is that my mum had packed many clothes in my box. Maybe she knew the clothes would serve as a blanket on this cold winter night.

Anyways, I passed my language exam, started University, changed course and schools about three times and finally graduated . . . After eight years of suffering, the time had finally come to reap the harvest . . . you know, start making some money, . . . start living the good life . . . Or so I thought!

CHASING AFTER THE WIND

January 2007. The job search after graduating from University was a nightmare. I was six months pregnant with my second child Jordan and couldn't wait to start sending out applications. I smiled when Father Thomas told me

"Laura, children need their parents. Stay at home and take care of the baby for three years before you can go to work . . ."

I thought he was crazy . . . no, no, no . . . I knew he was crazy. Seriously? Did he know what I had gone through to get that degree?

The sleepless nights, rushing to work at 5 am., cleaning the corridors in the student hostel, dozing off in the library, failing and repeating papers? No, he surely had no idea!

"Forgive him, Lord, for he knows not what he says."

. . . turns out God had to forgive me. Those three years were spent running after job interviews, writing and re-writing CVs, applications for PhDs and so forth, but nothing seemed to work. It was what the bible describes as *"chasing after the wind . . .",* Until that day when the email came. It was 27 May 2010.

"Laura, a company in Cologne is looking for a Food Analyst to do Antioxidant measurements. It is not exactly what you did in your thesis, but I think you can do it . . . call this number to arrange for an interview . . ."

And that is how I found myself signing a work contract on June 17th, 2010 to start work the same day. It was like a dream. Three weeks after Jordan's third birthday. That was the day I started believing that God still had prophets in our days. Father Thomas' words had been nothing short of a prophecy. What do you think?

LESSON ONE: GOD'S TIMING

Yes, God's time is indeed the best; because in His time all pieces of the puzzle fall into place. The ease with which I got that job indicated that it was God's hand at work.

How else do you explain that a company schedules an interview without even knowing the name of the applicant?

In fact, I gave them a copy of my CV after the interview. So, if you are trying too hard to get something and it just wouldn't work, you might want to take a step back and seek the Lord in prayer. He may be inspiring you to change course or hold on a little.

Has someone ever told you something ridiculous, only for it to happen years later?

Did you see it as a message from above or just a coincidence?

That is what was happening to me. The answer was right there, at the right time

So, I started work, and all was fine. I had my share of ups and downs, misunderstandings with colleagues, failed experiments, poor treatment and all, but all these changed gears when I announced the good news;

"I am pregnant!"

I will never forget the reaction of the Director's wife. Two weeks of silence and then she broke it with.

"Sincerely, I was very shocked when I heard you were pregnant. I thought you were done! One girl and one boy."

I only realised months later that what she was saying was that they employed me because I had two kids and had closed the chapter. But now that I decided to open it again? Needless to say, we must part ways. That was good and fine for me; I too was tired.

"Life goes on my people; In fact, I wouldn't want to work a day longer in such hostility."

My doctor must have read my mind as he looked up from his computer that day and said *"it's enough . . . you are no longer going there . . . "*

Yes, the situation at work made my third pregnancy tough. I wasn't sure how; but God saw us through and my third child Jayson was born, on our fifth Wedding Anniversary. Talk about comforting the afflicted. The smile of my baby soothed my pain. Though I enjoyed the maternity leave, I was excited to go out into the world again, have some adult conversations and inhale some chemicals. But alas! Baby Number Four- Jannis - was knocking at the door . . .

AGAIN . . . WHY ALWAYS ME?

Fast-forward - October 2013: I was going into a depression. Yes, it was hard. How could I be pregnant again? That was not the plan. I wanted to go back to work! But God had opened another door for me after I was kicked out by my former boss. Bless his heart.

Every disappointment is a blessing. Right?

I prefer to say *"an appointment with God . . ."* Anyway, I got the chance to start an internship in the *Food Security Office* in Cologne.

No! Do not tell me about God's plans. This pregnancy was a real blow in the face. That was it! Four kids?

My husband, Daddy Paul was working out of the country at that time and only came home on weekends.

How was I going to take care of four children?

Were all my years of studies going to waste?

Oh, how sorry I felt for myself.

I sat crying one day, thinking about all my friends who were pursuing their careers and all the smart couples who had one or two kids. I felt so silly because my heart was pumping with anxiety. It wasn't long before the stares and questions started coming . . .

"What? Are you pregnant again?

"What are you and Paul doing with so many kids?"

"So, you just wasted all those years in school. You surely can't work in the lab with so many kids, right?"

"Come on Laura, why did you do that? You should have taken care of that pregnancy. Gone are those days when people had a bunch of kids. It's not cool."

Yeah, it was hard. I felt like a criminal each time I stepped out of the door. Reminds me of a quote that has been attributed to former President of Zimbabwe, Robert Mugabe.

"Be nice to pregnant women. It's not easy walking around with evidence of having had sex." How right he was. Nonetheless, very few people seemed to obey him.

Do you know anyone who has many kids?

How do you feel about them?

Are you maybe in the same position as I was?

It was in the middle of my misery that I heard a voice saying . . .

"Why are you so sad Laura? Why all the tears and sighs?"

Laura: "Well, isn't it obvious? My life is over. Why me Lord? Why always me? Why does everyone else seem to have themselves under control?"

The voice: "So, you are crying because I have blessed you with another child?"

Laura: "Blessed? Why don't I feel blessed? Why am I not jumping up and down? By the way, did I ask you for another 'blessing'?"

"I have just one question Lord. Why did I have to suffer through University for eight years? Am I ever going to work as a Food Chemist again? Why did I waste all this time?"

The Voice: Haven't you always said you wanted to serve me with your life?"

Laura: "Well . . . yes!"

The Voice: "So, do you need to be working in the Lab to serve me?"

Yeah, I realised that all my talks about "being a handmaid of the Lord, going wherever He leads" were just lip service. I wanted to go, on condition that it was in line with what I wanted. Yes, I knew the Lord had lots of work for me to do. I had books to publish; I had conferences/workshops and seminars to organise. Yes, I was aware of that and wanted to do it . . . but on the side - as a hobby, not full time.

My strongest desire was to work as a Food Chemist. I wanted to be called a *"Karrierefrau"* (German for career woman). I wanted to adhere to the standards society had set for me. Yes, but God and his so-called "blessings" were standing in my way. Realising that He wasn't going to change His mind, I asked . . .

Laura: "But my neighbours are going to laugh at me. Remember the mean comments they made about baby number three, Jayson? How am I going to face them with another pregnancy?"

The Voice: "Laura, your neighbours are going to take this news the way you present it to them. If you are looking like you do now . . .

they sure will gossip and laugh at you. But if you are radiant, excited and happy, they will have no choice but be happy with you."

LESSON TWO: PACKAGE IT RIGHT

Wow, that was an 'aha' moment. But He was right. Most often people react to what we present to them. It was truly an eye-opener. That meant I had to change my perspective on this situation. The only way I could look radiant and happy was if I believed that this was truly a blessing. I had to believe that being a Food Chemist was not the ultimate and that I could still live a happy and fulfilled life without ever stepping foot in the lab again. That is how I learned the power of my thoughts. My smile gradually returned as I started thinking of myself as blessed. As I started thinking of myself as happy.

Do you agree? What role do thoughts play in your life?

I finally found Joy and peace again. I could finally brush off the mean comments and mockery from my friends. My husband and I welcomed our fourth child, Jannis in July 2014. What a handsome baby he was, real sunshine till this day!

How I wished I had learned this lesson in those early years in Germany. This would have helped me greatly when I changed University, but my life became a living hell.

Big-City Life

Oh, the nights I spent crying. The many times I sat sulking, grumbling, cursing and blaming myself for making the wrong decision. I was angry at God for not answering my prayer for guidance and protection, enraged at all around me for not stopping to mourn with me and disappointed at those I asked to join me in prayer for not praying hard enough.

September 2001: With a sigh of relief and a broad smile, I stepped off the train. *Willkommen in München!* (Welcome to Munich!) I could feel my heart racing in my chest as I imagined the exciting things that awaited me. Big-City life, here I come!

It was sad to leave all the wonderful friends I had met in Kaiserslautern (where I had studied for three years), those who had stood by me and taken me by the hand through the jungles of a foreign land. My Russian sister, Svetlana, my German brother, Alex and my Turkish brother, Turkan, who cried so hard, pleading, *"Laura, why must you leave? Why must you change universities now? Just two more years and we will be done. Please, please!"*

This was my song, inspired by Donnie McClurkin: "I've got my mind made up, and I won't turn back, because I've got to live the big life someday."

Yes, my mind was made up, and no one was going to stop me, not even my sweet Mama. Today, her words *"Lau, please don't go"* still ring in my head like it was yesterday.

"Life is all about making choices, Mum, and sometimes you need to let go of something to gain another." I packed my bags and off I went.

BIG-CITY LIFE QUICKLY BECAME BIG-TRYING LIFE.

Things turned sour after just a few weeks. My laughter soon faded into sighs as I felt my heartbeat swiftly decreasing.

Munich turned out to be a nightmare! I could not take it any longer, so I packed my bags and took off for Cologne. Barely six months later, I was off to Detmold. Cut a long story short; I finally found myself two years later in Stuttgart.

By now, Svetlana had obtained her master's degree and was working. I learned from her that Turkan was doing a Ph.D. The walls of my six-square-meter room turned black.

Thinking about how I had gotten myself into this vicious circle, making one wrong move after the other, "running from the frying pan directly into the fire." Could my 'wicked' uncle in Cameroon be behind all this? He wasn't happy to hear I was travelling abroad. I was very suspicious!

Need I say I had not moved an inch with my studies?

Around me, everyone seemed to be prospering. I felt like people were laughing. They were happy and excited.

Why? What was there to laugh about?

There was only one word I could spell:

"M-I-S-E-R-A-B-L-E."

"But, Laura, what was up with you? Why did you have to move so often? What exactly where are you looking for? Had you become an academic nomad?"

"I know me sef? Cha! I have suffered!" (I have no idea. Lord, help me!)

But in the middle of all this heartache, I realised that God was saying something. There is a prayer I have not shared with you, one that came up every now and then in my early twenties:

"God, I pray that someday You will bless me with a husband, a man who loves and fears You, a man who will love me like himself and take great care of our kids and be a wise and honourable man."

Okay, okay, you caught me. Guilty of plagiarism. That was my mum's prayer for me, replacing "me" with "my daughter."

My focus was elsewhere: "God, I pray that someday You will bless me with a loaded, tall, handsome and muscular guy who would make Denzel Washington turn green with envy. He will buy me the best shoes, clothes, and jewellery, not forgetting the sports car I have always wanted. He will take me to Mallorca every summer . . . "

Okay, make we leave am so! (Let's leave it at that!)

Have you ever found yourself in a similar situation? Could God be trying to talk to you in the middle of that storm? Anyway, let's move on.

So, was God guiding me at all? Had I been making the wrong decisions all this while?

Yes, at the time it felt so wrong. The pain was amplified by feelings of regret. Oh, how I wished I had stayed put. How I wished I had been meeker and listened to my sweet Mama. How I wish I had paid attention to the tears and pleadings of my dear friends. Oh, how foolish I looked even in my own eyes, not to mention the gossip, stares, and sarcasm that went around about me.

You may be reading this now and thinking *"Wow! I can relate."*

Has your Big-City life also become a Big-Trying life? Are you full of regrets for making the wrong decisions? Do you feel that God has disappointed you?

"A person's folly leads to their ruin, yet their heart rages against the LORD." Proverbs 19:3

I feel your pain. Though I went through hell, I see things today from a different perspective. As painful as it was, as hard as it was to believe, this was an answered prayer. A blessing. Let me explain:

Had I not changed Universities and toured Germany a little bit, I might never have met my husband, Daddy Paul, and would not have the wonderful life I am living today.

LESSON THREE: BLESSED IN THE STORMS

So just because I faced challenges and suffered, doesn't mean I made a mistake. Jesus suffered a great deal, but it wasn't a mistake, was it? My sufferings might just have been the will of God for me as well. That was how my mum's prayer for a God-fearing husband for her daughter was answered. Besides, I believe these hardships were necessary for God to prepare me for His plan for my life. Some lessons in life are only learned the hard way. Right?

So, my dear brother, my dear sister, keep the faith. Offer your pains and burdens to Him. Let Him grant you the grace to endure while He works things out for your good. Let Him bring out the message that is hidden behind all these trials.

Do you realise what healing a change in perspective can bring? Exactly what I needed in August 2003 when I found I was pregnant in University.

Oh! Why always me?

"YOU GET HEART" GOD BLESS YOUR HEART!

March 2005: He tried to hide it, but it was too late. I burst into tears as I stared at the little pink dress. I had just returned from Cameroon where I left my one-year-old daughter with my parents. The decision had been hastened by the lady at the German 'Foreign Office' who had refused to extend my student visa unless I sent the child away. She said I did not have enough money to sustain both of us, so one person had to go. Now that was a shocker! Three months before that, when I went in for my one-year visa extension, I was told I would be granted a five-year residence permit because my daughter was a European citizen. Wow! Talk about favour!

"The stress of the past year is finally paying off."

I thought, as I pushed the baby and danced my way back to the student hostel that day. I flashed back at those big tummy days. I had been the talk of the campus as everyone tried to guess who the father of the child could be. There were those who felt sorry for me and did not hesitate to mock and gossip, and there were also those who thought I was courageous, admired me and tried their best to support and encourage me. Some knew that I had forced the pregnancy in an attempt to get the 'poor' father to marry me. Some predicted that I was going to abandon school which was confirmed when I travelled out to have my baby. Oh yes, I felt like one of Mugabe's 'criminals' and carried the proof around with me. Guilty as charged!

However, I was more worried about the fact that my insurance company had kicked me out. That's what happens when you don't pay your insurance for five months in a row. Lord have Mercy!

How was I to see a doctor?

How was I to know that everything was fine with the pregnancy?

There were times when I believed God was punishing me for my sins. Yes, there were times when I thought this baby and his/ her dad were agents of the devil who had been sent to make my life miserable. Yes, there were times when I wanted to put an end to my life but for some reason felt concerned about that child. At some point, I even thought I was looking forward to having that baby. As I said, I thought.

Today, when I look at my 14-year-old daughter, I wonder where the years have gone to. A few days ago she gave me a pair of shoes her aunt had bought for her. They were too small for her feet. Yeah! Daddy Paul gets sometimes confused when I walk into the living room

"Who is in the kitchen? I thought it was you . . . hey, you ladies have to stop wearing the same clothes . . . "

Her brothers surely wished she was a little more lenient, but when it comes to it, they know they have a second mummy. I had mixed feelings one day when Jayson (six) said "Mummy, Shantelle makes better pancakes than you. She can cook better Mummy; we no longer need you . . ."

Yes, Shantelle's coming into this world was a challenge. Who would have imagined that I will be talking of five children today? I am so grateful for each one of them. So similar yet so different.

WOMEN EMPOWERMENT SUMMIT— COLOGNE, GERMANY

Most often people ask me:

"Five kids?

How do you manage to do all the travelling, writing, public speaking?

Isn't it tough?"

It's no secret that women are at times put in a box when it comes to having a successful career and raising kids. It's no secret that most women decide not to have kids because they want to pursue a career and achieve their goals in life. It's no secret that children are sometimes regarded as obstacles, preventing their mothers from going out of the house.

But is that always the case?

Is it possible to raise brilliant kids and still have a successful career?

The news of the pregnancy of my fourth child, Jannis left me in a very daunting position.

What were my chances of returning to working as a Food Chemist?

Were all those years of studies a waste of time?

Though it looked almost impossible, I knew deep inside me that I could still make use of my talents and education. I just needed to have Trust in God and believe in His power in me.

The Women Empowerment Summit was created to give women an opportunity to share life experiences on how to break loose from the mindset of fear, overcome challenges and *"take that leap forward."*

In line with the target mentioned above, this yearly Summit will benefit the participant in following areas:

Renewing their thoughts. To always believe in the positive according to Romans 8:28 *"And we know that in all things God works for the good of those who love him, who have been called according to his purpose."* Romans 8:28.

Pushing through to achieve goals despite the inequality between them and men, and the additional hardships and obstacles on the way. *I can do all things through Christ who strengthens me.* Philippians 4:13.

Making an impact in their communities by challenging themselves to do extraordinary things, according to the motto, "we are not staying behind" *"That is why we always pray for you. We ask our God to make you worthy of the life he has called you to live. May he fulfil by his power all your desire for goodness and complete your work of faith."* 2 Thessalonians 1:11.

Networking, sharing experiences and testimonies through best practices and successful examples to encourage one another. *"Let your light shine before others, so that they may see your good works and give glory to your Father who is in heaven."* Matthew 5:16. Recognising personal gifts and talents.

Partnering with and supporting other women to achieve greater goals *"As each has received a gift, use it to serve one another, as good stewards of God's varied grace."* 1 Peter 4:10.

"The aim of bringing women from different Regional and Religious backgrounds and still tackling issues that affect women was accomplished. We need more of such groups . . ."
                                          —Joy ZENZ. Founder, AWE

(Note: Cologne awaits you every year - August/September - for the Women Empowerment Summit. We look forward to networking with individuals, groups, and companies who would like to take this Summit to the next level. Contact me if you would like to sponsor or partner with us.)

MARRIAGE ENRICHMENT SEMINAR

One of the best things that happened to me was meeting my husband, Daddy Paul. Let's say the road was rocky at the start, but today I have a friend, brother, and partner in one. I think of him each time I stumble on Ephesians 5:25 "Husbands, love your wives, just as Christ loved the church and gave himself up for her."

This is not to say we have been giggling since day one. After 11 years of Marriage, we have had our fair share of challenges, disappointments as well as days (or weeks?) we would not exchange a word with each other. So what is it that has kept us together to date? How have we managed to overcome daily challenges of a marriage?

The Marriage enrichment seminar is the place where couples (and singles contemplating marriage) can sit down and talk. Workshops and exercises will allow couples to dig into real life issues and find solutions.

This yearly event will take place every summer in Cologne. Let us transform ourselves and our world. One marriage at a time. You are welcome to support and partner with us.

INSPIRATION FROM OTHERS

I will not be where I am today without wonderful friends and partners who have supported, rebuked, corrected and inspired me to be and do my best . . . I say, "thank you."

One of them is Joy Zenz, founder of African Women in Europe. I first contacted Joy in July 2017 when I was looking for sponsors and partners for the Women's Conference. I stumbled upon this lady on Facebook and sent her a friend request which she accepted almost immediately. A few hours into the day and she had confirmed her attendance and sponsorship. Talk about 'Rapid' results. I was impressed by her humility, selflessness, and eagerness to see others grow.

". . . next time you get a conference room in a hotel, Laura."

Yes, Joy challenged me to take the Women's Conference to the next level and, she saw something else in me that day . . .

MODERATING AT THE AFRICAN WOMEN IN EUROPE AWARDS 2017

Four weeks later, there I was moderating the African Women in Europe Awards Ceremony in Berlin, which welcomed over 150 participants from all over Europe. It was simply AMAZING. We had a great time.

Gosh, what can I compare it to?

"David and all the Israelites were dancing and singing with all their might to honour the Lord. They were playing harps, lyres, drums, rattles, and cymbals." 2 Samuel 6: 5

That is how it went down in Berlin. That's how I felt each time someone said "Wow! You did a great job. You are an awesome moderator. You made us laugh; you made us feel special . . ."

But guess what! I remember when she asked me to moderate the event, I was like . . . "What does this woman want from me? First . . . organize conference in the hotel, now . . . moderate the Award show . . . ah ah!"

"dem send you for ma back?" ("Please give me a break!")

Of course, I was SCARED! Oh goodness me! Yes, I have moderated and talked to groups of about 20–30 people but 200?

> ### *"No no no! That is too much. I can't! What?*
> ### *In a HOTEL? No way"*

But I heard the Holy Spirit asking me *"Why do you think you can't do it?"* Though I had all the reasons, I came to realize that there was actually NO reason at all. I was the one trying to convince myself! I was the one placing limits on myself. It was all about my thoughts and mindset. Then I remembered a verse from Luke which says:

". . . for the Holy Spirit will teach you at that time what you should say." Luke 12:12

Oh yes! That gave me hope. I was just an instrument in God's hands.

Needless to say, "God did a great job." As I stood on that stage, I realized that there was just no difference between talking to 20 and 200 people. Guess why? It is because it's the same Spirit. It's the same God.

LESSON FOUR: YES YOU CAN.

You may be at a point in your life right now where you are limiting yourself, and you convince yourself that you are too small. Are you buying into the lies from the enemy that, that thing is a number too big for you? "No, you can't go there . . . it is for the BIG people . . . You have just a little oil."

No, no, no, let me tell you now . . .

You are big! You are a child of the King. You have royal blood flowing through your veins. You have been well equipped. Say to that enemy in your head: "if one person deserves it, then it is me! It is the same God. And if He can do it for A, B, C . . . , then He can do the same for me!"

My life has been far from perfect – actually, it's a daily struggle to survive. As soon as one thing is sorted, the next one pops up – leaving me no space to breathe at times. As much as I can't change the situation I have learned a few things which help me soar in the middle of the storms. With your permission, I will share these top nine tips with you:

1. **Prayer**

   There are times in my life when a situation arises which seems very critical. I panic, I make phone calls, I grumble, I curse, I cry, I frown. I push blames, I regret! And the last person I want to see at that moment is God. Yeah, because I hold Him responsible for my situation. "Doesn't He have all the powers? Why didn't He stop this? Why doesn't He help me? Why doesn't He change my story?" You too?

   But after all, this, when I finally gain wisdom and decide to pray . . . there is just some indescribable peace that comes over me! I calm down.

   When I calm down, it is not because the problem has been instantly resolved! No, sometimes it even gets worse, but because I have prayed, I know that Jesus is now in control. I know that I no longer have to fight that battle alone! I know that there is a power above all powers which is acting in my favour! I receive the solution by faith. I know that He has already rebuked that wind and raging waters. The storm has subsided. It is all calm. I am calm. That, to me, is true healing!

2. **Honesty**

   Another thing I have learned is the power of honesty. Being honest with myself. Being honest with others. The first part of solving a problem recognises that there is one. The chances that I have missed in life because I tried to deny the fact; deny my fault; deny my weaknesses, and deny my helplessness.

3. **Humility**

   Honesty requires first that I am humble. The bible is very particular about humility.

   "God opposes the proud but shows favour to the humble." James 4:6

   Another famous quote says

   "Pride goes before the fall."

   It's not easy, but by God's grace, I am learning to fight this vile – pride - in my life and replace it with the virtue of humility.

4. **Ask for help**

   One of the ways pride can cause you to fall is that it deceives you that you are all sufficient and can do it all alone. That's a big lie! The reason why I so love the AWE motto *"Together We are Strong."* After struggling with this for a very long time, I am enjoying the benefits of asking for help. Admitting my weaknesses and working together with others for a better tomorrow.

5. **Respect for the opinion of others**

   Working together means respecting and accepting the opinion of others. Knowing that you cannot always be right and that God will also use others to teach, correct, rebuke and train you in accordance to His Word . . . why . . .

   . . . so that the servant of God may be thoroughly equipped for every good work. 2 Timothy 3:17

   As much as I always want to have things my way, I have realised the importance of paying attention to what others have to say. And most often, I have found the solution to my problem by so doing.

6. **Forgiveness**

   I have come to realise that many times my problems are amplified and aggravated because I have unforgiveness in my heart towards someone.

"Lord, how many times shall I forgive my brother or sister who sins against me? Up to seven times?"—Matthew 18:21

I know what it means to forgive someone over and over, and that person just keeps doing the same thing. Seven times? That should be the maximum right?

Jesus answered, "I tell you, not seven times, but seventy-seven times. Matthew 18:22

It may be hard to believe, but if you want to live a victorious, peaceful, successful and amazing life, you must be quick to forgive and move on. Remember

And forgive us our debts, as we also have forgiven our debtors. Matthew 6:12

And of course, apologise and ask for forgiveness when you have offended. Right?

7. **Choose your fights.**

"You will never reach your destination if you stop and throw stones at every dog that barks."—Winston Churchill.

We live in a free world with a diversity of opinions and freedom of speech. Sure, there are times when you need to clarify and defend your opinion. However, you must know when to ignore. Pray and ask God for wisdom.

8. **Believe in yourself.**

You are much stronger than you imagine. Be willing and open to trying new things, take risks and delve into the unknown.

9. **Golden rule**

"Do unto others what you want them to do unto you . . .", Enough said!

Consider it pure joy, my brothers, and sisters, whenever you face trials of many kinds because you know that the testing of your faith produces perseverance. *Let perseverance finish its work so that you may be mature and complete, not lacking anything. James 1:2-4*

FAMILY EQUATION BALANCED

In closing: I can't end this chapter without talking about my child-hood, family, my mum, my siblings, and the blessed life I had in Cameroon, without which I would not be me.

Dschang–Cameroon, 1992: My aunt put down the phone and shouted . . . *"The baby is here."* That was great news, but we were more interested in another detail: *"It's a boy!"* that is when I broke into dancing, inviting my sisters to join me.

"Equation balanced. Equation balanced . . ."

Rewind nine months: I had been very annoyed when my mum told us, we were getting another sibling. Was I like *"Seriously? Another baby? You must be kidding, right? You can barely take care of 5 of us; you want another baby?"* My sisters Lidwina and Lesley couldn't agree more. The boys Emmanuel and Cletus though too young to under-stand, sensed that there was something fishy going on. Yes, things were rough in the country at that time. 'Economic crises' and 'deval-uation' were making headlines.

I was in boarding school and could barely afford the things on the list. Mum became an expert at making things out of soya bean - milk, cake, bread, etc. So, yes, we were not really excited about the coming of another child. I remember mum telling us one day *"you know, the child is going to come. There is nothing you can do about it now. But once he or she is here, I permit you to do whatever you want to do with the baby. Throw it away, flush it down the toilet . . . you decide . . ."*. Huh? Now that was shocking! As much as my siblings and I were not excited about it, getting rid of the baby was the last thing on our young minds.

We couldn't get enough of the baby Paul aka "popo" once he arrived. He was sunshine. He did not only balance the equa-tion, three girls, three boys; he balanced many other things in our hearts.

Six years later: I remember crying my eyes out as the car drove off to the airport to catch my flight to Germany leaving my six-year-old brother, Paul in the yard. His red square shirt and a deep blue pair of trousers wet with tears as he waved at the car. His words *"I am going with Laura to Germany"* kept ringing in my ears. *"I will come back and take you . . ."* I had told him, wondering if he even understood . . .

Did I even understand where I was going to and what awaited me?

ONE (OR TWO) FOR THE ROAD

My dear brother, my dear sister, thank you so much for stopping by to read my story. I pray you have been inspired. Life is a journey, and we are walking together. We need to be each other's keepers – holding hands and helping each other along the way. There are times in life when I have doubted my existence. But somehow, I always saw the light at the end of the tunnel. Keep the fire burning. You are more than Conquerors! With Love and Blessings.

Dr. Gianluca Zanini

I am a 50-year-old Italian male medical doctor who specialises in radiology. I was born in Italy. I was adopted by a fantastic couple, who have been my parents since I was 3-year-old. They also adopted my two sisters. I now live in The Gambia, Africa. I am one of the few male members and supporters of the African Women in Europe Network.

I have always been engaged as a volunteer in educational activities with children and young people and later with international students' associations. I became a doctor in 1994 and was dreaming of finding my way back to Africa, The place where I had travelled with my family as a child in 1972. My love for Africa has to lead me to meet African people during my travels and all-around Italy and Europe, discovering cultures, traditions, and experiences. I appreciated how empowering African people are.

I have an 11-year-old son, who I love dearly.

Occupation: Freelance specialist, Medical Doctor, Radiologist

Area of Expertise: Healthcare, Hospital, Medicine

Interest: All aspect of Africa, culture, history, traditions, people, problems and future development.

Books: Co-Author: African Women in Europe (supporting male)

Contact Details:

https://www.linkedin.com/in/gianlucazanini/ https://www.facebook.com/gianluca.zanini.7

Twitter: @GianlucaZaniniD – Skype: gianlucazanini

Email: gianluca_zanini@hotmail.com

Phone: Gambia +2207454723 / Italy and WhatsApp +393442991901

Chapter Four

☙

GOING TO AFRICA; IT IS AFRICA CALLING YOU

By Dr. Gianluca Zanini

INTRODUCTION

"Open your heart to Africa, let your heart beat to Africa rhythm. Africa will open up to you and let you dance to Her rhythm."

I decided to write a chapter in the Perfect Migrant book to tell my story as a **'European Man in Africa.'** I know my story will shock many because it is not what you expect. Here it is, I hope you enjoy reading it as much as I enjoyed writing it.

I began to love and explore Africa when I was only five years old, thanks to my father who took the whole family, with my mother and two sisters, to visit Morocco for the first time in the far 1972.

Since then, I have travelled continuously for over twenty years far and wide across the Sahara, living true Africa life, not the touristic version, meeting peoples, cultures, traditions.

After a 20-year break, I started traveling again in Africa in 2014. I moved to the Gambia in April 2017, giving life to my African dream that was in my heart since childhood.

For more than a year my heart has once again opened to Africa.

In 2015, I was introduced to an association for women AWE by an African woman named Lucy whom I met in Switzerland. In fact, she brought me to the African women in Europe Network and to participate in the Lausanne conference in Switzerland. I will write more about this experience later in the chapter.

Learning from those who, starting from different parts of Africa, had made their journey to Europe, bringing with them their own experience, culture, traditions, problems, and the greatness of Africa, in its diversity and incredible human richness.

"To know their values and principles was invaluable."

I met women of the incredible strength of character, with personal human experiences unimaginable in Europe, with a wealth of soul and character difficult to find on a continent like Europe, where in some ways everything is available and possible, guaranteed and protected.

Encountering these powerful African women represented for me was an important moment of personal growth, of knowledge and also of a better understanding of what my life project could mean, the value I could give to it, and also more knowledge to help in my decision to move to Africa, wherever life and work would bring to me.

It was that defining moment that made me think; I could develop important, strong, deep friendships with women from different African nations.

So, I stayed in the network and volunteered at subsequent conferences. I have met and known many more friends during AWE conferences or in other meetings during the last few years. They have helped me with their knowledge, their advice, their information.

I have not always been a good "student," and often I have not carefully listened to advice and suggestions, especially of the most cherished African friends. As a result, I have made some mistakes in my assessments, despite everything.

But who has never made mistakes of ingenuity in his life?

And anyway, I brought with me, in my heart, their words, their teachings, the advice, the friendship and the affections, keeping in touch even from afar.

All these aspects of my life, my experiences with Africa and the African people, my love for Africa have led me to participate in this amazing adventure of the AWE book. I write this chapter for whoever wants to make a move to Africa. Later in this chapter, I give some suggestion and encouragement from the lessons I have learned.

But first, I want to pay tribute, my respect, and gratitude to all the AWE Ladies and to all African women who with their lives and souls have taught me a lot as I build my future in Africa. I also thank you reader for taking time to read my story; I hope you will find fun and value in it.

FAMILY

I'm Italian, and I'm 50-year-old, but my spirit is very young. When I think of Africa, when I talk about Africa, and much more

when I am in Africa, I feel all the energies and the enthusiasm of my youth.

Love and Marriage

Since early 2016, I have welcomed the love of a young African woman, Faith; she is from Uganda. Uganda is also known as The Pearl of Africa. Faith has chosen to follow and share my dream step by step. We are walking along the path of life together.

We met casually on Facebook, talking and sharing our common interests for each other's cultures. Day by day we found a mutual interest, attraction, and love. Despite the big difference of our origins and stories, we found amazing common aspects of life and mutual interests. Then the day came when we decided to meet and share real life, to live together and to build a life together.

In September 2016, I finally flew to Kampala to meet this beautiful woman. Her country welcomed me, making me immediately feel at home, in my Africa.

The second time I went to Kampala was in December 2016, and I stayed there for one month, living the Christmas Season and the New Year Eve with my lovely Faith, traveling around the country, visiting places, meeting members of her family and friends, enjoying every moment together. When I moved to the Gambia in April 2017, she joined me in June, and since then we are living together, building our relationship and strengthening our love. We finally got married in February 2018, celebrating the Kwanjula, the traditional Ugandan wedding, and then the court marriage. That was our dream coming true and the real beginning of our life together and our family.

My Son

I can't forget a very important person in my life: I have a beautiful 11-year-old Italian-Dutch son, Xavier. He mixes the best part of the Italian and Dutch cultural heritage, and he will become a great man.

I am so proud to be his father. He lives with the mother, my ex-wife Fleur, who I enjoy a wonderful and respectful friendship with.

DOCTOR ON A MISSION TO AFRICA

I am a medical doctor radiologist and have been working in public hospitals for twenty years, with experience in various countries such as Italy, The Netherlands, Switzerland, and more recently, The Gambia.

"I wanted to be a doctor since I was a kid."

Above all else, my dream was to become a missionary doctor in Africa, to leave Italy for any part of Africa where my services would be needed. To spend all my life as a doctor at the service of the most disadvantaged, those who are failed by the system and could not receive assistance, and to help those with the big and small diseases of life.

"Life, the real one, often has its projects and its obligatory steps." Or rather, as those who have faith say, God has His plan for us and knows when the time is right for the choices and the direction that we must follow. In fact, my work went very differently from what I thought.

After graduation in October 1994, I worked as a military doctor in Italy. Later, I specialised in radiology.

In November 2000, I started my career with my first job in an Italian hospital.

In 2003, I found a job in The Netherlands that led me to move for the first time to live and work abroad. However, after one and half years, at the end of the contract, I returned to work in Italy.

In 2010, I went back abroad, this time moving to Switzerland where I stayed until the end of 2014.

Once again, life wasn't quite what I had expected, and so I moved back to Italy to work. I stayed in Italy from the beginning of 2015 until last April 2017.

In almost twenty years of work, I have changed nations, cities, hospitals, always looking for that inner satisfaction that seemed never to arrive, despite the magnificent working conditions, cutting-edge technology, and a decidedly high salary. Something was still missing in my life.

In 2014, I began to turn my search for a new job to Africa, to those countries that I knew better or which I had contacts and friendships that could give me advice, information, and help.

Finally, in April 2017 I moved to start a new life in Africa. I am now working in the Gambia, a small country in West Africa, tucked in the Centre of the largest Senegal. I work in two different clinics, one is a private clinic, and the other is a non-governmental organisation (NGO).

Of these clinics, the one that attracts me the most is the NGO clinic which was created in July 1990 to provide medical and educational assistance to Gambian women of all ages. The clinic is called Bafrow Medical Centre, which is in the heart of the city.

Here I have contributed my expertise as a radiologist at the launch of the first mammographic screening program for breast cancer prevention that, together with other cancers, in recent years is becoming an increasingly widespread medical problem even in Africa.

It is not easy to work in the field of diagnostics, where expensive machinery is needed, of high technical and scientific value, and many years of experience to be able to often interpret very complex images and give the meaning and value of what the doctor can see.

To this must be added the big problem that, unlike other medical and surgical specialties, diagnostic machinery are often missing, or they are very old and almost unreliable, and above all, they lack the necessary funds to replace the obsolete machines or even buy the first stains.

Here is a challenge;

To use all my knowledge, my skills, but also all my enthusiasm, sometimes courage, and the will to carry forward a project of work, profession, and life, and to be able at the end of the day to say:

> *"Today I helped a patient, trying my best to answer to his health needs."*

To better understand the reality in which I find myself today, and how I got there, we need to take a long step back and see better of where this story started.

Throughout my youth, I have always had a romantic idea of this dream, due to reading books on the experiences and lives of those who had gone on a mission in the past or meeting those who were still missionaries and came to Italy to tell the stories of their lives in person.

Growing older my commitment began in the activities of religious groups that were involved in missions. Missionaries and their support, up to the university period, participating as a medical student in the training courses of the CUAMM in Padua (University Center for Aspirant Missionary Doctors).

At the time, it was clearer what it meant to leave for a mission as a doctor, even if it remained a difficult goal to achieve.

It meant that first of all I had to be professionally prepared. To gain the knowledge and skills suited to a completely different medical reality from Italian or European.

Above all that bringing my work to a vast and different continent like Africa, meant being ready to adapt to a thousand different possible situations.

"I would have to adapt to Africa, not Africa to me."

Unfortunately, after university, my life began to follow decidedly different paths and often in the opposite direction of my dream.

Family aspects also influenced the direction of my life, because when you share your life with other important people, you must do your best for them, even if that means to find a different place for your previous dreams.

So, the marriage, the son coming, the job that takes the time, many things, needs and daily decisions that take their time and attention and, perhaps, they came before every dream.

However, I did not stop thinking about Africa, and although everyday life absorbed almost all my mental, emotional and physical energies, I kept thinking about Africa, discussing with friends and colleagues. Talking to people who lived or had lived in Africa, whether it was a doctor, a priest, a professional or a simply a volunteer, and the nostalgia of the years of my youth spent traveling in North Africa came back fresh every day in my mind as if they had been the previous summer's trips.

Meanwhile, time passed, and life took a direction different from any prediction, because it touched first the affections and bonds of the family with a painful separation and divorce, and then my career that suddenly stopped with the end of the previous contract.

I found myself with no work, no family, no friends and with some health problems, all within a few months. I did not have a social or cultural life, and all this was happening in a foreign nation, Switzerland. Everything seemed to collapse around me.

MY AFRICAN FRIENDS SAVED ME

I joined a group called the African Women in Europe (AWE). This group was introduced to me by Lucy, a friend from Kenya, who was part of the network and I was experiencing a difficult time in my life. Lucy and the other women and men I met helped and supported me, with their friendship. Lucy's affection and her knowledge of Africa and African people made me want to go to Africa even more.

With her, I discovered the magnificent richness of their different cultures, traditions, experiences, motivations, projects.

I began to contact hospitals in several African nations, in the hope that one of them had the need and the possibility to hire an Italian radiologist.

One after the other I looked for hospitals in Kenya, Uganda, Tanzania, Botswana, Namibia, South Africa, even Saudi Arabia, which of course is not in Africa.

Alas, the time passed, and the work did not arrive, not even in Switzerland, where I had lived for some years. I even tried in Italy, England, France, and Ireland.

I did not even get responses from any of the hospitals that could turn into a concrete job and life opportunity. I sent two proposals to two private clinics in Botswana, in the end, were also not conclusive.

An interesting parenthesis was the New Year Eve of 2014–2015. After 21 years of distance, I have finally had the opportunity to return to Africa. I went for holidays in a tourist village in Egypt.

At the same time, a proposal from Italy arrived, It was from a hospital where I knew the head of the department. He invited me to join him to work with him within that hospital. So once again, project Africa was postponed. At least for the time being, life was better.

I needed a salary, to get myself out of a difficult and painful situation I found myself in Switzerland, which was not taking me anywhere. I accepted the job in Italy, although always with the intention of continuing my search for my way to Africa.

Two years later the work in Italy finished, and still, I did not find my road to Africa nor a new job in Italy.

Nonetheless, at the time something important happened in my private life, one of my deepest sentiments. Faith came into my life, and into my heart bringing me, at least for one step closer to my dream of being in the heart of Africa.

It was her beauty, heart, and personality and not the fact that she was from Africa, that drew me to her, though that helped, because I knew that it would bring me closer to my African dream.

The place I loved and dreamed since childhood. The one that in my eyes has always been the true destination, Africa.

The land where ebony is the colour of life, and the place that soon would become my life, even if at the time I did not know it.

HOW I LANDED IN THE GAMBIA AS DOCTOR.

A new phase of my life, the one that would take me to Africa for the first time as a doctor and no longer as a traveller, to start a project to recover a small hospital founded by a doctor from The Gambia and open new health care service.

It all started when an Italian doctor, whom I knew for working together in Switzerland, gave my name to a Gambian doctor who, while working in Switzerland, had founded a private clinic with attention in a remote part of the city, which was original, entrusting the German wife with the direct management of the clinic.

In the clinic, he invited European doctors to commit themselves as medical directors and administrators to manage the whole activity for variable periods of time.

Not having been a director for about a year, as soon as he learned that I was passionate about Africa and looking for work in Africa, he contacted me and, with great enthusiasm, proposed to me to be the next director, bringing my professional experience, my passion, my experience of management and development of the clinic.

Obviously, it was an important and huge choice. I tried to learn as much as possible about The Gambia, about the culture, the clinic, and about the doctor who had contacted me. I discussed it with friends in Europe and Africa who knew me well and could understand if I was suitable and ready for this big step.

On the other hand, the time was very short, and I had a long hospitalisation before departure. It did not facilitate the high level of preparation I needed.

However, I was perhaps more supported by the desire and enthusiasm that a real preparation for the difficult task that awaited me, above all the great changes in life and, not least, the risks that this choice meant: success or failure?

Despite making the first trip to learn about the hospital, at the most serious moment of the national political crisis due to the fall of the previous dictatorship, and after a period of illness that almost blew up all the plans, finally at the end April 2017 I left for Banjul, Gambia, to start what is my first real experience in Africa.

Everything seemed to be going well at the beginning, the difficulties of the climate, the different culture, the religious environment, the unknown language, the habits of life and work did not seem to be problems impossible to manage and overcome.

My experience of many years of traveling in different North African countries, the many friendships with African women and men of different nations, the support of their words and no less than my family and Italian friends and colleagues, all made me feel the strength to face any difficulty with a light heart.

Once I arrived in The Gambia, the positive and welcoming attitude of the staff of the clinic and of the people I met on the street was also a great help, giving me a greater sense of tranquillity and trust.

However, as the saying goes, *"not everything that glitters is gold,"* and after a short time, problems came out.

Needless to say; I lost my job after a month. All after I had invested passion, time, emotions, commitments, and even money.

Within a few days, I found myself in an unexpected situation, out of work, no income, with expenses made and to be made. I had no clear idea of how I was going to resolve the situation. It was an emergency, and I didn't know how I was going to organise the future.

All this with the daily threat of losing even the use of the house and the car that was given to me for my work. I was facing a threat of having the police and the immigration office intervene against me. Thanks to the friendships I made with some doctors in The Gambia and with the girlfriend who had just joined me from Uganda to be by my side despite the negative changes, I was able to pull through eventually.

There were reasons to be depressed and worried, not only for me but also for the woman I loved and who had chosen to live alongside me despite the difficult moment.

There were moments when I thought of giving up everything, returning to Italy, even without work or home, giving up the dream and surrendering to a reality for which I had not prepared myself.

I think that many in my place would have surrendered and would have returned home with the pain of defeat and the breaking of the dream. But, I am a tough head.;

> **"I make my mistakes; I take the responsibilities and consequences of my choices and my actions."**

With the help of my girlfriend, who bravely decided to stay by my side, to fight with me to resolve the situation, to live in poverty if necessary, I decided to stay in The Gambia and find my way here. I chose to fight to build my professional position. I was ready to even if it meant changing jobs, abandoning the profession of doctor, and opening a business that could give me a chance to maintain our lives and build a family, but always remaining in Africa.

I was not ready to abandon my African dream.

The situation and possible developments are easier said than done, but anyway, with a little effort, I slowly managed to recover.

Using my savings, I did some calculations, and I worked out that I could stay in The Gambia safely for a while, even without earnings, while looking for work in some private clinics or trying to open a business with my girlfriend.

So I bought an old car, I found a rented apartment, and I started to look for a job again, introducing myself in several private clinics.

At the same time, I started writing a project proposal for modern and complete radiology to be presented to the Ministry of Health, to be built with the collaboration with the ministry, the University of Banjul and foreign sponsors and donors.

After presenting the proposal to the ministry and writing a Memorandum of Understanding, in reality, everything fell silent, and even today as I write this story, it is months later, I have not received any official contacts, despite my repeated requests.

On the side of my doctor's work, the first positive effect was seen at the end of July 2017, when I started the first talks with the director of a private clinic interested in my expertise as a radiologist.

I am happy to write that in August 2017, I started working as a consultant in a clinic known for the quality of work, for good doctors and health workers.

Of course, the work is still little, but slowly people are becoming aware of my presence in The Gambia and my job, and they come to the clinic to have the examinations I can perform.

Meanwhile, life also continues at home building step by step that strong and deep relationship with my now fiancée Faith, which is leading both to an even-deeper relationship of love and laying the foundations for the future family.

It is great and important to have the help of the person who loves and understands you, supports you in the good and difficult moments. The bonus of her being African helps me to understand the Gambian culture better.

However, hope is always the last to die and so, as for The Gambia, hope for me is also resistant.

NOMINATION AS A MALE ROLE MODEL

First, I must say that a wonderful surprise that filled my heart with emotion and pride, in this long period, came from a completely different reality, but that is strongly connected to my association and belonging to the association of African Women in Europe. They contacted me to tell me that I had been nominated for the award of Male Role Model. This was the first time the association has decided to honour men for their commitment and support.

You cannot imagine how beautiful and important this news made me feel, it was such an honour.

> *"Me, a man, a European, considered by African Women worthy of recognition as a role model!"*

Although it had nothing to do with me living in The Gambia. With all my problems and disappointments, such news brought me a lot of strength and confidence at a difficult and challenging time.

I did not win the prize, the actual award, but nomination itself to me was like winning the first prize, and everything else did not matter.

So, between the search for new work, the arrangement of my situation in the Gambia, life with my girlfriend, in September 2017, I went to a conference in Berlin, where I once again met many African friends, and I made new friendships.

From Berlin, I travelled back to Italy to visit my family and to arrange some documents. While I was there, I received another surprise, this time from The Gambia.

A Gambian woman doctor had received my name and contact from an Italian doctor who runs a major African research centre located in The Gambia, and they needed a radiologist, she did not hesitate to call me.

There it was, a new chapter of my medical career and my work opened in the Gambia. My perseverance was paying off.

As soon as I got back to The Gambia, I went for the interview, and we started collaborating, opening the mammographic screening project for breast cancer prevention, for the first time in The Gambia, and once again an important personal involvement with African women.

In December 2017, I received a further surprise: I was contacted by a Gambian woman who lives in London to collaborate with a new health project that will deal with the prevention of prostate tumours in The Gambia and seek doctors to start the research, diagnosis, and therapy.

This means a new commitment in the health field in a nation that needs to rebuild itself from the past and build a better future for all Gambians, and I hope in some way to make my contribution, leaving something positive and valid for future generations.

When I look back at my life, at what I have built in my family, social, professional reality, I realise how many changes and how big they have been.

When I was young and still at the beginning of my career as a doctor, thinking to myself:

"Someday I will go to Africa."

Many things seemed different, in some simple and linear respects:

First step; to study and become a doctor.

Then study the problems of the mission as a doctor in Africa.

Then look for the organisation with which to start my medical mission in Africa.

The fact of having grown up as a Catholic, and believing so deeply, gave me strength and determination to pursue my ambition, but at the same time, I did not realise that many aspects were not clear to me or even I did not consider them. This attitude, even if in good faith, led me to grow in a non-homogeneous way and therefore not to prepare myself in the right way to reach the necessary maturity.

The result was to disperse the mental and emotional energies, without being able to reap the fruits of my commitment.

Even from feelings and love, that leads to getting involved with a partner to build a relationship and then a family; all this have certainly had great weight in diverting my attention from my original goal.

More than once, I heard from the partner that I wanted at my side:

"if you go to Africa, I'm sorry, but I will not follow you."

And then it is not easy; once you find the person to love, who shares your feelings, with which you build a family and have children, you can't just say *"ok, I will leave everything behind the shoulders, and I go to Africa."*

Surely one thing I understood now is that:

To completely change your life, especially to achieve a goal, it is not easy, nor fast to do. It is achievable with determination and perseverance.

We need to plan our time, our actions, the steps and the intermediate stages to be achieved at the right times and the right ways.

And you need to learn as much as possible, talk to those who have had similar experiences, especially with those who want to go where you want to go. Because it comes from that reality. We grew up, know the flaws and benefits, human and cultural mechanisms to be able to enter that reality from a right direction and in a correct way.

MISCONCEPTIONS ABOUT AFRICA

The most common misconception I have encountered in Europeans is the idea that Africa is a unique social, cultural, political, historical, human identity. To be honest, as a European, a little of this mentality is also mine, at least unconsciously.

"Nothing could be more wrong than this simplistic and decidedly ignorant way of thinking about an immense continent like Africa, with a variety of incredible cultural, historical and social wealth."

However to my advantage surely are the decades of experience of travelling through Africa, crossing many nations, knowing personally the peoples, cultures, traditions that are part of it, and for this I have to thank mainly my father, who since 1972 has decided to share with his wife and children an incredible love for Africa and the Sahara, giving me a significant openness compared to my peers who have never left Italy, or even the village where they were born.

Every country that I have visited, traveling, have had contact with the people, has its characteristic, different and specific ways of approaching life, of welcoming the stranger, of opening or closing one's heart to those coming from outside, a different measure of morals and ethical values. These can also change enormously from one country to another.

Being European, well-off, with a very high professional and scholastic education, with years of experience in their work, does not represent a guarantee of being accepted and succeeding in Africa. , especially when going to Africa with a sense of superiority and arrogance because they think of coming 'from a civilized, rich, advanced countries'.

The knowledge of foreign languages is another important obstacle, and it is not at all certain that knowing English or French is enough to get in touch with the locals, despite the centuries of European domination that has imposed the use of European languages on local languages.

In fact, the "normal" people, the one who lives in a difficult and different reality every day, have not always had the opportunity to study and often have not learned the foreign languages, although these have been official in their respective Nations. This can become an obstacle to communication and also mutual acceptance or can create mistrust and rejection.

Another great mistake typical of foreigners, especially Europeans, is the idea that arriving in an African country with money, ready to invest even huge amounts of money, to open factories, commercial offices, farms, industrial facilities, is the best method, because "money opens all doors."

In reality, the most frequent outcome is that the company becomes bankrupt. Because often behind the capital, no efforts are made to study the cultural and social realities of the country one goes to invest. Since often the economic conditions and realities in Africa are difficult or ruined by the corruption of the politics and the bureaucracy, many Europeans end up becoming prey to cheating and theft, resulting in the loss of capital, businesses, and sometimes even lives.

There is, however, to say that on the other side of this accepts a widespread prejudice across Africa and the first people to raise my awareness are just my African friends in Europe and Africa. The idea that the white man is rich, whatever he does or he says or his age, he is a plucking chicken.

Of course, compared to the average African person the white man, or rather the European or the American, is richer. The fact that a white man could travel from his country to Africa, and able to afford exotic holidays in another continent and then go back home, does not necessarily mean that all Europeans are rich or rich enough to throw money out of the window.

In short, at the end it can be said that when you start a journey, a goal, the realisation of a dream, there are fundamental aspects to keep in mind to avoid making mistakes or at least to reduce them to a minimum, to engage your human, emotional, financial, temporal resources and get the most from this commitment.

LESSONS I HAVE LEARNED

"Investing in a life and work project is not just about investing money, but above all investing one's emotions, expectations, knowledge, time, feelings, human and family relationships."

1. It is essential to be invested. We must be ready to pay all costs, whatever they are, and accept any risk. The possibility of reaching only part of this project, to commit material and human resources sometimes unpredictable and even higher than the initial calculation, to achieve a totally different and sometimes even more important goal, to totally fail and find yourself forced to start over.

2. We must take into consideration every aspect of the problem, of the project, of the various stages to be achieved, of the way that leads it to success.

3. If for one reason or another, you decide to move to Africa, you must first of all be clear of what Africa represents to you, which Africa you want to go to live,you must learn, study, know the particularities of the Nation in which you want to move to, of the population in the midst of whom you want to go and live and work with.

4. It is equally important to know people who come from those lands, make friends with them, open your heart, ask questions and listen to answers, because those people can give you immense cultural heritage and provide you with the knowledge that often not even the most important books and courses can teach you.

5. In this sense, the humility and simplicity of the approach are really important and effective, breaks down barriers first of all cultural and social, but also historical, considering the sensitive nature linked to colonisation despite several decades since the end of colonialism.

6. Even learning the language of the Nation is important, but not always easy or possible staying at home, and it will surely be a winning choice to take the time to study at least the basics. Once you get there, once again relying on social relationships and the natural welcome that every people have for the foreigner who strives to learn the local language, regardless of the nations involved.

But when you only speak about money, you enter a territory much riskier and with greater chances of failure. Because money, especially if you have a lot of it, attracts all kinds of people, first thieves, and cheaters.

All sorts of scams are possible around every corner and at every moment. This is because those who bring money to invest make the mistake of not making a proper assessment beforehand and because often the trickster thinks that "this investor has so much money that I can enjoy with too."

This specific financial and commercial situation, therefore, requires considerable attention and preparation on the part of anyone who wants to go to Africa to invest. It is very important to have a deeper understanding of the local economic situation, and also the ability to adapt the investment to this reality, also modifying the projects and working methods, but even modifying the product, the commercial target, the production or the distribution of the product, to adopt the entire investment to a reality very different from the European one.

Nonetheless, above all you should not give blind trust to one person, perhaps the first arrived, you must listen to more voices, more proposals, and evaluate the one that has more credibility and shows greater seriousness.

We must also be very careful about where the money goes, who should receive it and who wants to intercept the path for personal gain.

This attention must also be given to projects involving humanitarian actions, where perhaps scams, corruption, and abuse are even more frequent.

FINAL WORDS

I would like to conclude this chapter, the story of my experience and the considerations that have arisen with some simple advice, without claiming to have the truth and with all the humility possible.

Taking the road to Africa is not at all difficult or impossible when strength comes from a profound conviction.

From valid human and even spiritual values, from an accurate technical and cultural preparation.

From a humble awareness of one's limitations and from accepting advice and suggestions, and also from teachings from those who have more experience.

Both because they come from Africa, and because they have already experienced first-hand the path that they are about to undertake.

My Top Survival Tips to the European on Going to Africa

First, be humble, accept your limits and learn to recognise the limits of your project, no one is perfect in this world.

Be ready to invest everything including yourself with conviction and be prepared to accept the risks that are always present in every human reality.

Inform yourself as much as possible and prepare yourself to the best, so that you are not surprised by the unexpected or errors of assessment. Be mindful that you will not be protected or immune from errors, but at least you can prevent or solve the major difficulties, knowing that a part of the uncertainty is always there because Life itself is uncertain.

Learn to know and recognize the value of Africa and Africans, their rich human, spiritual and cultural heritage, but above all learn to give yourselves to Africa.

It is only through giving yourselves, your heart, your spirit to Africa, with gratitude and generosity that you will in return receive the greatest gift that Africa has to offer. The same way your generous mother gave you your life.

"I have a deep passion and love for Africa. I am also a male member of the African Women in Europe network."
—*Gianluca Zanini, Author.*

"When the deal is too sweet . . . Think Twice!"

Angelinah Boniface

A mother, wife, daughter, sister, auntie and a friend. I consider myself a transformational leader, life coach and a trainer at heart. I am also a keen listener and learner.

My passion is to equip, guide, impart knowledge and skills to all those who are at crossroads in whatever part of their life journey, such that they can re-discover their passions and inner purpose. I believe that each one of us is here for a unique purpose. My journey is, therefore, to try to raise that deeper awakening within us, to align people with their life purpose and leave a fulfilling life, positively impacting communities. All this requires unique commitments from each one of us.

I cannot live another person's life, however, what is satisfying is seeing others go along their journeys with contentment and entertaining as big expectations as they deem possible.

Books Include: (1) Co-Author of The Perfect Migrant (2) Celebrating Diversity.

Area of Expertise: Motivational Speaker, Human Rights Defender.

Speaking and Seminar Topics: Overcoming Your Shadow Vision.
Contact Details
Phone: +1 646 894 9964
Email: Angieakaboni1@gmail.com

Chapter Five

☙

BORN A MIGRANT: MY STORY, MY PRESENT

By Angelinah Boniface

INTRODUCTION

"My story: Born an immigrant, education and poverty reduction."

My journey of thousand kilometres into the Diaspora where I rediscovered myself began on a day in September 2007 with a few steps from my beautiful mansion mud hut in Moroka village, in the North Eastern part of Botswana. I had gone home to bid farewell to my mother and my siblings.

This is a cultural cum religious practice in most African societies when a person is about to embark on a journey, especially to a destination afar and unbeknown to many. I had secured a place and a Commonwealth fellowship to study for my masters at the University of Sheffield, United Kingdom.

My mother, who is a very prayerful woman, prayed for me until her voice faded. She was praying for my protection. In her prayer, I could sense her fear and reluctance to my going. This is the power of prayer, where our hope ends, grace takes over. This was my mother's prayer. She did not understand why I had to go but prayed anyway.

At the end of the prayer she looked me in the eyes and said; 'my daughter, I have prayed, you have made your decision. You want to go into a jungle. I fear for you, but God will protect you'. She was oblivious to the poverty surrounding her. Probably because we were poor but very happy. At that moment I also started crying, tears rolling down my cheeks. I could hardly lift my feet as I was trembling at the thought of leaving my children and my family behind going into what my mother had described as a jungle.

The earlier, excitement of studying for an MSc in information systems abroad disappeared. Tears continued rolling down my cheeks. I asked myself a question; are there places where Angels fear to tread? For, I consider myself an angel. With no immediate answer, I decided to leave everything to the Almighty God whom I believed had sanctioned the journey. I stepped farther away from the compound reflecting on my beginnings, my family, my life and my future.

I was determined to pursue further studies. I was convinced that after obtaining a masters degree, I was going to be more marketable. Get a decent job and kick out the poverty that was characterizing my family. The mud mansion hut where rituals were performed was an eyesore and a sign of glaring poverty. I was determined to break the patterns and pathologies of poverty and thought in my family.

There was a pathology in my family which I was now part of, grandmothers raising their grandchildren without any involvement of their father. Here I was, about to embark on a journey leaving my two children with my mother. My grandmother raised my mother's children in Zimbabwe. My mother raised my sister's children. In each instance, the father of the child had little or no involvement in the child's experience. Motherless children more often will grow up and feel abandoned. Grandmothers who become surrogate parents are most often very overprotective. I see this with my mother today in her relationship with my son.

I was born Angelinah Cynthia Boniface on 21st January 1983 in Moroka village to poor migrant parents. My parents had come from Zimbabwe then Rhodesia, a country that shares a border with Botswana. My grandfather who was a co-founder and prophet of the Gospel of the God Church founded in the 1920s. He had left Zimbabwe in the 1950s on a pilgrimage that took him, his four wives, children and followers to Kenya, Tanzania and Zambia before settling in Botswana. To this end, migrating was not a new phenomenon in my clan. It is in my family's DNA.

FAMILY AND RELIGION

My late father, Shadreck Mutero Chandiwana was born in 1939 in the Royal family of the Chandiwana clan in Mahusu village in Chikomba district, Zimbabwe. My grandfather Hodzeri Boniface Mutero Chandiwana missed the opportunity of being installed as

Chief Chandiwana upon turning to Christianity and embarking on a pilgrimage before settling in Botswana in the 1950s. His Christian believes did not allow him to become a chief. Nevertheless, he remained part of the royal family, so was my father and me.

At the age of sixteen, my father, His Royal Highness Shadreck Mutero went back to Zimbabwe and reunited with the Mutero Chandiwana family in Zimbabwe. It was a way for my father to reconnect with his roots. He later rejoined his parents in Botswana in the late 1970s fleeing from the war that had broken up in Zimbabwe. My father and his siblings never went to school. He was never formally employed. However, my father was home taught to write his name. He could count and account for his money with the rudimental counting skills.

My mother was born Leya James (Nduku), 1949 in Shurungwi, Zimbabwe. She got married while very young. At the age of 26, she had four children. She also was never formally schooled. The husband was very abusive. She later left him and went to work as a housemaid for a white family at a farm in Mount Darwin leaving her four children in the custody of her brother Timothy Nduku. In the early 70s, my mother also fled from Zimbabwe at the zenith of the liberation war in Zimbabwe and sought refuge in Moroka village in Botswana. She escapes because black people who were employed by the white farmers were regarded as 'sell-outs.' In Botswana, she met and married my father. Four of us were born out of the union. I am the third born.

Life as a little girl in Moroka village in the 1980s and 1990s was beautiful. Not rosy, but I was happy, and there was a lot of love. We were poor yet delighted. What a weird combination. Everything revolved around the church. My family belonged to a religious sect mentioned earlier co-founded by my grandfather. All the sect followers, the Bazezuru lived in one big compound.

The church elders propagated the notion that we were God 's favourite people. They would brag that 'we are pure and not supposed to mix with the 'gentiles.' This exercise of control made sure that we all belonged and were loyal to the sect and its practices. The church leaders choreographed all aspects of life. Worshipping in the compound was a daily routine. There was limited time for the people to fend for their families. As a result, the sect followers could hardly afford the basics including decent accommodation. Our family was not spared. The future for many looked gloomy.

However, according to the sect's philosophy, everyone has to be entrepreneurially utilizing the time when they were not in group prayers. The saying goes like 'God will multiply by several folds what you get at the end of the day.' It seemed nothing multiplied. Admittedly, they worked hard but not smarter.

The returns remain limited. When is the multiplication going to be realised? This is the multi-million-dollar question. The male congregants in the church were engaged in making basic household wares like hoes, axes, pots, and baskets. Their spouses would sell the wares in our village and the neighbouring ones.

That was my father's earlier occupation. The men were also engaged in menial casual jobs that were not paying decent wages. At any rate, they did not have any formal education let alone technical qualifications. My parents and others have agricultural plots from where we grow crops mainly for subsistence.

Around seventy percent of school-going children were not going to school. Those who fell sick were prayed for instead of being sent to the hospital. People would die in their houses. The situation was made worse with the advent of HIV and AIDS. Teen mothers with malnourished babies were all over the compound. They had not been to school; early marriages of young girls and polygamy were a norm.

I recall, at the age of seven, an old man brought chocolates to our homestead and said to my parents; *"these are for you my wife, Angelinah."* Such was the courting methodology that was seen as 'normal.'

The worst of the practices was a female genital modification. This is a practice where a young girl's genital area is modified through cutting, to suit her future husband. I am a victim of it.

I recall severe pain, bleeding profoundly and crying following the pulling of my labia . . . I was only ten years old. The irony is, my mother never told me to do this. However, the pressure from my peers in the compound let me do it. It was expected of me, so I thought. While crying, I committed to fighting against this practice.

I vowed that I would never subject my daughters to any genital modification, let alone force them in to marry a person they did not choose. I also vowed to pursue education and get a job that will enable me to take care of my parents.

One day as I prayed, I wrote on a piece of paper about my dreams, buried it under a rock and hoped that one day God would answer my prayers. One of the dreams I recall very well was, "work for WHO, the World Health Organisation." Growing up, I found the only international organisations I could easily pronounce and remember were FAO and WHO. Hence I aligned myself with them.

EX-COMMUNICATION FROM THE CHURCH.

My father was against the practices in the church. However, he had limited choices. He had grown up in the church. He had become one of the elders. Consequently, he was expected to be leading by example. At the same time, he wanted to lay a good foundation for his children. For the latter to happen, it meant he had to disregard the cardinal principles of the church.

He decided to send his children to school. His actions were against the cardinal principles of the church. They were therefore taboo. The church elders continuously harassed him. He was not allowed to participate in meetings concerning both the church and the welfare of residents in the compound.

The final, act was his excommunication from the church in 1990. My father was considered rebellious by his people. Our family was ordered to leave the compound. This was heartbreaking to him for being separated from the people he had known his entire life. I was in 4th grade when the eviction took place.

The events of the day are still vivid in my mind. I remember I was coming from school. On approaching the compound, I saw my mother clearing grass and small bushes from an area close to the mixture. I was so touched, and I started to cry. The compound had become my place and my world away from our supposedly home in Zimbabwe. That Zimbabwe home was in my father's 'talks' to us.

He often reminded us that we are part of a royal family some-where in Chivhu in Zimbabwe. It was home in abstraction until I visited it later in my life. It was like what mother Africa is to the African-Americans. It exists in their dreams. Many of them have never been to Africa. In a fit of anger, I told my mother 'we should go home in Zimbabwe.'

The news of the banishment was not all that welcoming. It almost shattered my hopes of a better life. I concluded that 'we have been ostracised we are now outcasts.' I began to think seriously about my identity. I had to ask myself whether I was part of the Tswanas or Zezurus. The former were exhibiting xenophobia tendencies, and the latter had rejected my family.

As a family, we started building our new home with limited resources. It was not an easy task. My parents did not have enough money to buy new building materials including cement for mould-ing durable bricks and hire a builder. We had to use second-hand materials. All of us had to contribute in one way or the other. From school, I would get home and join my mother in moulding rudimentary bricks using mud. My father, as a self-taught builder was responsible for constructing the huts being assisted by my brother.

I recall after we had built our homestead, grandmother used to come to spend the day with us before going back to sleep in her hut in the compound. There were no adequate huts to accommodate all of us. Initially, we had two huts. One thing which touched me most was the poor roofing material. The old asbestos sheets had holes and were not properly secured. Stones were put on top of them.

Our huts stood distinct from others because of the stones on top of the roofing sheets. The stones became the identity of our homestead. During the rainy season, the roof leaked. The stones were often blown away when it was raining and windy. I recall one day when coming from school I found the roofs of the huts blown away. However, slowly though, my father kept improving the huts as resources became available.

The expulsion taught my parents to worship God in a congregant that is tolerant and open enough to embrace societal changes. As a family, we joined Saint Marks church. It was also a wakeup call for him. He became independent and became more resourceful. He started to work a bit smarter. Our new home ended up being home to the Saint Marks church. People came to our house every Sunday for the church. By the time my father passed on, our situation had improved a lot. However, we remained poor but going to school.

EARLY EDUCATION AND ADOLESCENCE

I was a bright pupil and an envy of many in Moroka village. My father always bragged about. He attended all my sports events and prize giving. My father loved me dearly. At school, my teachers were proud of me. I also developed a positive attitude to education while I was in primary school. However, the 'poverty element' in our family was visible. My parents could not afford to buy extras beyond the prescribed school uniform. Poverty became a source of the bullying that I experienced at school.

I recall in 5th grade, 1993, one pupil from a rich family, Boemo Maripe bullied me by attacking me, my father and our poverty. She drew in a piece of paper, my father as a poor man with a gap in between his teeth; she mocked our three mud houses that had stones on top of them and circulated this paper around the class.

The drawing stuck in my mind as I grew up. Apart from the mockery, Boemo disliked me because I was smart and the teacher's favourite. The mockery became the source of inspiration for me to work out of poverty. I resolved to put more effort into my school work so that after school I would get a job and build a nice house for my parents.

Apart from school work, I was also a good athlete and a class monitor or perfect at all stages of my schooling from primary to high school. I used to enjoy the responsibilities. I would wake up in the morning in high spirits looking forward to going to school. With my friends, for middle school, we walked a distance of about four kilometres to and from Ramoja junior school.

'We cracked jokes and playing on the way.'

At home, I was also happy especially when in the company of my young sister Lebo who was born when I was ten years old. She was cute and lovely such that I always looked forward to going home after school lessons to be with her.

I graduated with flying colours in the junior and high school. I was the first in our family to graduate. My elder siblings had not graduated. Through pressure from society and the environment, they decided not to pursue further education after elementary school. Our cousins and nephews who were part of the sect were not in school.

> *"I believe that the environment around us can influence the decisions we make in life. Such was true with my elder brother and sister."*

INSPIRATION TO MAKE IT IN LIFE DENTED

While in high school, Masunga senior school, 1999 April, disaster struck. I got pregnant and had to drop out of school. During the Christmas vacation after middle school, I had visited my elder sister in Francistown. I used to visit her when on holidays.

There I met my first love. He loved me dearly he would do anything for me. At fifteen we made out. I fell pregnant. The news not only shocked my family but my community. My parents were devastated. They were elders in the new church, Saint Marks that we had joined upon being expelled from the Gospel Church.

Our church like others does not condone sex before marriage. I was a disgrace to the church and a laughing stock in the community. On seeing me, with anger, my mother remarked 'my daughter you have brought shame to us.' She could not stand me and walked away. My mother did not speak to me about all my pregnancy.

My inspiration to make it in life was dented. My dreams of building a house for my parents had suddenly vanished. My vision of breaking the intergenerational poverty could no longer hold. A new reality of a teen mother was in the offing. I could not stay in the village let alone with my mother who was bitter and shouting at me all times. I had to go and stay with my elder sister and her family in Francistown. My mother did not visit me while pregnant, but my father did. I cried controllably when my father visited me. I could feel the urging of telling him what I had envisaged doing for him and my mother that which is no longer possible. Build a house for them.

On 6th October 1999, I gave birth to Ashley Goitseone, my son. It was the best day of my life, and yet the scariest. I love my son. He was the best thing that happened to me. I became a teen mother. It came with its harsh consequences. I began to ponder about how I was going to take care of this baby.

> ***"Does it mean I have to sell vegetables in the village
> market to raise money for the upkeep of the two of us?"***

We were poor, and it meant my child was destined to be poor. I was to pass on the poverty to my child.

There is a saying in my mother tongue, *"nhamo haibve paneimwe"* Literary translated as 'poverty doesn't come to an end.' In essence, it's about inter-generational poverty. I struggled with the idea that we were poor, and that I had brought a child into this world, as poor as I was. Again, all my dreams had been shuttered. I decided to seek salvation from God.

One day, in January 2000, I woke up early in the morning. I went to pray in the mountains. I went straight to the rock where I had buried my dreams. I began to pray; in fact, it was more of weeping than praying. I wept till I lost my voice. In the process of praying my breasts started itching. At that point, I remembered my son must be crying. The mother-child connection! I needed to go home to breastfeed. I rushed home having resolved at that moment; I will be going back to school.

The journey to find a school that was admitting dropouts began the following day. My former high school denied me re-admission. Dropouts are not entertained. With the determination to get back to school I went to the regional education offices in Francistown.

At the Offices, I met the regional education officer, my former English teacher, Mr. Zibani. I was confident that he was going to assist me since he knew my potential and from our village but alas! No help came from him. I was devastated. A lot of things came into my mind. One that was positive was for me to look for a daytime job while going to a night school.

I began looking for a job. I would leave my child with my sister while getting into town. I would come back midday to breastfeed the child and return to town in the afternoon to continue with the job hunt. The routine went on for weeks. The first week in March, as high school opened for new freshman, as I sat under a tree breast-feeding, I saw Dudu, a cousin to the father of my child. Dudu is slightly older than me. She had dropped out from school under similar circumstances. To my surprise, she was putting on a school uniform. After the exchange of the usual niceties, I asked her about her school.

*"My cousin told me that Francistown Senior School
is now admitting dropouts. The next day I went to
the school and enrolled."*

I went back to the village to leave my child with my mother. I started senior school staying with my sister and later on with my aunt. I would go to the village during the weekends and the holidays to be with my child. It was hard, but I had no choice.

Within two years I had graduated from senior school. I passed senior school and got a place to study at the University of Botswana. Once again, I brought joy to my family. My mother was proud. I was the first in our extended family to be enrolled at a university.

UNIVERSITY EDUCATION AND MY JOURNEY INTO LIFE

Apart from the lectures, I had the time of my life at the university. I had fun. It was like I was being born again. I had an allowance, and that made it easier to take care of my basic needs and those of my child back in the village. I made friends easily and mixed with colleagues during my time at the University of Botswana, bearing in mind my background as a young mother.

I had no relatives in Gaborone, the capital city. This meant a limited interaction with the outside world except for my new church, the Old Apostolic Church of Africa. I was either in school, church or hanging out with friends. At church, I became a Sunday, school teacher. I used to enjoy the moments I spent with the children during the Sunday schools. I began to appreciate the role of morality in life as it was an integral part of the teachings to the children.

University learning went smoothly, and I graduated with a first class in 2006. This is the first class that was to earn me a place and fellow to study for a Masters in Information Systems in Sheffield, United Kingdom (UK) under Commonwealth Scholarship marking the beginning of my journey and life in Europe. The year was 2007.

For me, the year 2007 was a turning point in my life. Apart from the fellowship, I gave birth after a difficult pregnancy to my beautiful baby girl, and also, secured an interview with the United Nations. In February of 2007, I had sat down for the United Nations National Competitive Examination in Gaborone, Botswana that was followed by an oral interview in August at UN office in Geneva, Switzerland. Following the interview, two years later, I was offered an opportunity to enter the UN Secretariat in New York in 2009.

I was overjoyed when I received the news that I was selected for a Commonwealth scholarship to study in the UK. Once again, déjà vu, the excitement disappeared on the day that I went to bid farewell to my family as I did in the introduction of my story. I was leaving behind my two children whom I adore very much. They were young, and the girl was only four months old. However, I needed the courage to step out from the village into the darkness to rediscover myself and start a new life with a future.

I had left the village before, not once, not twice but thrice. First, I had left the village as a pregnant high school girl. Secondly, when I went back to high school. Third, when I went to the university in Gaborone. I needed to break the chain of intergenerational poverty associated with my family. According to my mother, I had just graduated from the University of Botswana; I was supposed to get a job and take care of my children, get married and be normal or rather real.

She had no idea about the job market, let alone the competition among graduates over the few available jobs. I was still to secure a job, let alone a decent one. This gave me the strength to increase the steps away from the village to Francistown then Gaborone. I flew off from Gaborone to Sheffield via Johannesburg in South Africa into London, Heathrow before finally landed in Manchester, UK. The second time is flying; it was not one of the nicest flights for me as these issues continued to occupy my mind. I found myself crying during the flight. At one time, I had to visit the bathroom to cry so no one could see me.

THE UK AND REDISCOVERING MYSELF

When I landed at Manchester Airport, in September of 2007, it was a beautiful day. I was sunny and very warm. The University had arranged a meet and greet occasion and a bus to Sheffield. The ride on the bus to Sheffield University takes about an hour or more. This was the most exciting ride I have ever taken through the hills and the British countryside. I had never seen such beautiful green landscapes. This was the first time I felt the guilt of leaving my children and my family fading away. I was convinced that I was in the right direction, on the road towards the creation of a better future for them and myself.

None in my family had ever been to places like this before. None had flown before. I was the first to obtain a university degree, let alone to fly overseas. A Masters degree was about to come my way. I envisaged more occasion of being the first coming. As we got off the bus, I headed to the International Students welcome desk for my welcome package. I later phoned my mother and my sister that night to let them know I had arrived safely. My mother had been worried, and hearing from me was a relief to her. Although she pretended to be fine, I could tell she just needed me home, have a job and take care of the children.

"Settling in Sheffield was tough."

Everything from school to life after school was tough. Everything I knew about growing up in society was thrown out of the window. The culture shock was daunting. It was like I was learning a new language, a new way of doing things. It was a question of being socialised anew. People minded their businesses with limited time to socialise. The smiles were fake. In fact, they were not smiles but grins. I came to detest those grins since they were not well meaning. From where I come from people do not grin. In fact, they laugh till they cannot laugh anymore. I was in a land where I was to whisper everything. Screaming is a taboo. I could not laugh the way I used to laugh; otherwise, it was tantamount to making noise.

When I was home in Botswana, I was pretty happy; I had friends around all the time. I didn't know how to make friends, because friends are not made. Friendship happens naturally. When I went to the University in Botswana, my best friend, Keatlaretse Tubego, was a girl I met in the queue as we waited for our sponsorship letters. We didn't work hard to become friends, it just happened. In no time we were buddies. Even in high school getting friends was not a big deal. At my aunt's place, I stayed with three cousin sisters and six nephews. Ironically, I am still wondering how she coped with the numbers. Again, at our home in the village, there was no shortage of people to talk to. There was never a dull moment. I did not use to struggle to have people to hang around with.

In Sheffield, it was a different story. There were no friends and no family members. I was no longer the shy type. I was ready to make friends, but I did not know how to go about it in a new environment where people talk and respect personal space and boundaries. I had to take the initiatives against all the odds. I became close to two Nigerian students.

Was I looking for Nigerian friends?

The answer is no. I was looking for real friends, people from Sheffield, none came along. It was the environment that drew me to my Nigerians sisters. Three years later, I learned not expect too much. I had had my expectations too high. As tough as it was, my Nigerian friends, pulled me through to graduation. It was not easy, but we made it. However, I later made very close friends like Richard Campos. Richard is from Sheffield and married to a Burmese woman. I met Richard when I was working and interned at his firm, seconded by the University.

I thought leaving in a foreign country would be easy, just not in this world. Integrating took a toll on me. You are on your own. Even those you think are your friends because they probably come from the side of the world where you come from, are sometimes not genuine. In metaphoric terms, loneliness became my only dependable friend during my first days in Sheffield, though I could venture out occasionally. It was also getting severely cold getting into November. At any rate, I had not been exposed to snow conditions before, considering that my village was within a subtropical desert climate where it is mostly hot.

Loneliness became the norm most of the times after the lecturers. I had limited friends during my first Christmas in the UK. In the UK just like elsewhere in Europe, neighbours are not usually friendly or approachable regularly like in Africa. Granted, a neighbour is not necessarily one's friend, but in Africa, some bonding between and among neighbours usually develops. There is a huge difference between the African and European setups. In Africa, one's neighbour is as good as friend or relative. When there is a function at your place, the neighbour has a legitimate expectation to be invited. More often, no invitation is needed. You will walk into a wedding or funeral and ask later, "who is getting married or who died." Such is the beauty of our culture. It sounds strange, but that's the African way of living. This practice is more pronounced in the villages. In urban areas, this setup is fast disappearing as more and more urban dwellers adopt the western style of living. In Europe, the emphasis is on a nuclear family, and a neighbour is someone who is remote.

I remember getting a Christmas card and chocolates during Christmas holiday in December 2007 from my neighbour Andy. The card and chocolates were deposited in my 'letterbox'. The card did not bore my name instead it was addressed: 'Dear neighbour, 123 Litchford Road, wishing you a Merry Christmas'.

I had seen Andy in the corridors, had seen him leave and come in from work every day for four months. I had never heard his voice. Not even a hello from him. But here was Andy sending to a new neighbour, a Christmas card, and chocolates. The sight of chocolates and a card on my floor on my 1st Christmas from Andy has stuck in my mind to today. All my life I was surrounded by people more so on holidays like Christmas. The village comes to life during this time.

From football tournaments to weddings and parties, it all jovial. On this Christmas day, I found myself alone, empty and lonely. It had snowed on the hills of Sheffield. I had never seen snow before. 123 Litchford road sat on a hill; I stared through the window to admire the snow. I had no plans to venture out. No family, no friends. I was alone. It was indeed the saddest Christmas to date.

Loneliness can either drive a person insane or kill them. It was not going to kill me. Rather I began to search deep within me the meaning of purpose in life. Why am I here? How did I end up in this cold, grey place called Sheffield? It was then; I began the journey to self-discovery and awakening, find the true meaning of purpose of my life. Purpose, vision, and mission became important to me as I read around the subject. I concluded that a purpose in life has to start first with a vision and a mission. What is that you want to achieve in life for yourself, your family and indeed for the society at large? I was determined to change my life and to provide for my family.

The biggest lesson was learning the British culture. I embraced diversity. I began to understand the stereotypes associated with the British as my circle of friends expanded to include my host. I was rediscovering myself by learning also from others. I also learned a lot about how as Africans in general and African women, in particular, relate with one another in Diaspora. I was exposed to the challenges that are faced by women of African diasporas in the communities that they live in including the abuses perpetrated on them in their marriages.

MY ACCOMPLISHMENT AND THE RETURN JOURNEY

I completed my degree and proceeded to an internship. It was during the internship and during the times when I used to causal jobs as a student that I came into contact with working class in the UK. I had to cope with the workplace issues that migrant women workers face. These range from subtle racial and sexual discrimination, unpronounced segregation of young female migrants to disguised employment relationship characterised by indecent working conditions.

I remember walking into the office on my first day, and the lady at the reception pointed at the garbage can. She looked at me and said something like the can is behind the door, meaning I was there to collect the garbage. I politely proceeded to tell her that, my name is Angelinah Boniface and it's my first day of internship. She looked at me in shock.

For a year and a half, I did not see my children, my mother, and my siblings. I would call every day. I spent a significant percentage of the stipend money I received on calls checking on my children. While in the UK, I had managed to build a modern house for my mother, using part of my stipend money and money from part-time jobs. I managed to fulfil what I had vowed to do when my schoolmates were ridiculing our huts whose roof sheets were secured by stones. Changing the face of our homestead was my priority number one. The dream came true.

I only wish if my father, my departed hero, was alive for him to have lived in the house that her beloved daughter built. After graduation, and finishing my internship, I headed home, back to my village, to my children, my family, and a new house. When I eventually left the UK, I had rediscovered myself. I was ready to start a new life, a life with a defined purpose. Education turned around my life. I am a celebrated somebody in my village. It was a journey well-travelled.

"Education plays a significant role in addressing poverty."

The vision of my father, the sacrifice of my parents to educate me from their meagre resources and my determination to pursue education despite being a teen mother paid dividends. To all the teen mothers who think all is lost I say;

ARISE AND GO BACK TO SCHOOL

"Education is the tool to use in redeeming yourselves."

Through it, you can plan your destiny and destination. More importantly, it is the sword that fights the poverty traps that are associated with us the African women in the villages across Africa where we are selling vegetables at the marketplaces and in the Diaspora where the majority of us are doing menial jobs.

"Let us have more of the Angelinah stories."

Pamela Mahaka

I am 37 years old and a mother of one originally from Zimbabwe but currently settled in the UK for the past 17 years. At the present moment, I am working but have swapped my full-time job for a part-time job with the view to be an entrepreneur completely.

I have a Masters in Development Studies and a BSc Hons in Occupational Therapy (OT). I have been practising OT for a year and a half, and within that time I have mainly based my practice on private organisations.

Books: The Perfect Migrant: How to Achieve a Successful life in Diaspora.

Company Name: Independent Lives Therapy

Independent Occupational Therapist

Area of Expertise: Occupational Therapy—mental health and home adaptations

Contact Details

LinkedIn: www.linkedin.com/in/pamela-taurai-mahaka

Phone: 07557687441 and 01216499479

Email: pmahaka@gmail.com

Chapter Six

൫

THE GREATEST VIRTUE OF ALL

By Pamela Mahaka

INTRODUCTION

*"Defying challenges and achieving the impossible.
Breaking the glass ceiling in a foreign land."*

I believe that the greatest virtue of all lies in defying challenges to achieve the impossible. It is difficult to have dreams and not be able to achieve them because of the circumstances stacked against you. More so when you live in a different country from that of your birth. But how do you break these stakes without feeling like you are fighting an endless fire and burning out, and finally risking the passion that once gave you that inner drive? I have an answer, don't use the 'circumstances stacked against you' as an excuse to not achieve your utmost best in life.

VALIDATING YOUR WORTH

**"If you were born without wings, do nothing
to prevent them from growing"**
—Coco Chanel

As human beings, in life, we try and surround ourselves with friends and family so that we are not alone at those special events so that we have someone we talk to on a daily basis and also when we have a crisis. We clog our contact lists with their names but how many times have we picked up that phone, had a conversation with those people and thought *'oh that was judgmental'* or *'that was very unnecessary'* or *'I don't know why I rang you or speak to you anyway.'*

We confine ourselves to social norms which dictate that if we don't have a certain number of friends on our birthdays, then we are lonely.

But out of the 200 people or so who turn up on our birthday parties how many are supportive of our professional riches and career progressions?

In this short life of mine, I have noticed that people turn up for celebratory parties or any gatherings to compare the shortcomings in our professional and personal careers. However, I always ask myself why, as achievers do we surround ourselves with people who will celebrate our mere downfalls?

I may know the reason why. It is because in some instances we use those people to leverage us into pushing us and release that inner fire to prove them wrong. However, the same can be said for mentors.

I remember years ago when I was in high school, the third year of my first four years I failed my exams, and I knew I had failed before I left school for the holidays. So, I redirected the mail to myself instead of sending it to my mom's address. My uncle who is five years younger than me went to pick up the letter from the post office and took it upon himself to open the envelope which had my results in it. As he passed through the fields where myself and my grandma were working, he shouted from the road; mom (my grandma). Your granddaughter is so dumb she can't even pass the year three high school simple exams. She still has year four to go, and at this rate, she won't even get to England!

I tell you she will spend the rest of her life ploughing the fields with you on this farm! That's exactly the reaction I didn't want. Hence, me redirecting my results to myself. I was so embarrassed that I started crying. My grandma looked at me and said: *"now that you are crying what's that going to change? Dust yourself up and hold your head high you still have one more year to go to prove to yourself you can do this."*

That is exactly what I did. Passed my year four and went on for A' levels. I didn't even lift a finger on the farm after my A' levels because my mom sent me to the United Kingdom.

Years later as I have established a new network of friends and family in the UK, it was a difficult transition. I could not transfer my Zimbabwe qualifications into UK qualifications, so I started taking short courses, different NVQs and CPDs here and there. That was on top of battling for my residency to be approved. So, for ten solid years, I accumulated short courses and voluntary work certificates while facing an unknown world of going to be returned to Zimbabwe if the UK Home Office was to decline my application.

Once a friend of mine (who is also from Zimbabwe and lives in the UK) told me a story about how she had enrolled for a short course with a local college in the UK. She had asked her auntie she was then staying with for some money to supplement her course fees. My friend could not afford the fees as she was not allowed to work because she is awaiting a decision for her permanent residency in the country from the UK Home Office.

My friend reported that her aunt's response was;

"I haven't got any money. Drink water and bread and fund your own course."

She further said she had always felt like she was living in a world of uncertainty about her residency, her aunt's response left her *"feeling deflated and wanting to give up"* as she started to *"doubt"* her abilities.

As for me as soon as my residency papers came out, I applied for a master's degree in Development Studies, and by chance, I was accepted without me holding an undergraduate degree. This was just before the UK university tuition fees were increased from circa £3000.00 per year to the current circa £9000.00 per year. I tried to apply for development jobs in the UK as well as abroad. However, I was not successful.

Most of the jobs required one to have worked or volunteered overseas for at least six months. Nonetheless, I could not go for six months, abroad, unpaid or to be on any wages which would be below minimum wage. I was now facing four siblings back in Zimbabwe to autonomously educate, feed and clothe as my mother had by now passed away in a tragic car accident.

I was forced to reconsider my options.

THE BIRTH OF MY CHILD

In the final semester of the final year of my Occupational Therapist degree, I was pregnant. I know, (*perfect timing*). The course director told me that I could not take my final placement as it fell within the month I was due to give birth. She told me to defer. The whole semester from September 2015 – July 2016 and defer it to September 2016 –July 2017.

I asked for an alternative she told me there wasn't any. I told her that I was not going to accept that because in life there are always several options. She told me that even if I were to come back, I would not be strong enough to take on the final modules and a summer 2016 placement. I told her that that was my choice to take and if I was to fail it was only me to blame. I remember seeing her raising her eyebrows of doubt and me telling her that was exactly what I was going to do. I gave birth on the 28th of December 2015, and unfortunately, a natural birth turned to emergency caesarean section.

Classes were starting on the 5th of January 2016, so I missed that week of introductions, but the following week I was back in class. Fortunately, I was only attending one day a week. So, I had a lot of time to recover. My caesarean section would split with the walking I was doing, and I would come back and book an appointment with the nurses who would patch me up again. There were days when I would put the child to bed and sit up into the night doing the assignments. A few months after that I was a qualified Occupational Therapist. I acquired my first ever salaried job soon after qualifying.

> **"Success is never final; failure is never fatal.**
> **It's courage that counts".**
>
> **—John Wooden**

I had people who were willing to give me volunteering, training and mentoring opportunities; I was going to steal their time. I was going to sit next to them in the high profiled meetings. They were going to send me to those exhibitions, I will establish network links for them, but I will gain my confidence and continue with my resilience.

NEVER SURRENDER; YET WALK AWAY

Life in a foreign land is never easy. Some folks may say that it is easy to settle in another country – yes that could be true. However, there is another road where settling is not that easy. Where fighting for every milestone takes away all the passion and zeal.

But don't give up.

> *"Never surrender. Walk away and find another*
> *route to achieve your dreams if you must."*

If you hold fast to your dreams and ambitions, there is never one route to success.

Why am I looking back on these experiences?

Because past experiences have dictated the person, I am today. In these experiences, people have not celebrated my shortcomings, but they have criticised them, and that gave me the inner zeal to throw my fist in the air and want to prove them wrong and shout 'I can.' But alongside criticisms, I have always had a mentor who has supported me, and I have always called them my 'Air Punch Guides.'

When I am throwing my fist in the air to aim high, they have supported me to keep that fist in the air until I have all the tools of success in a row. I have had people saying, don't look back, but to me looking back is good. Otherwise, I won't have a baseline for my achievements. I succeed because we I surround myself with people who matter. I am who I am because of what other people have done or said to me, productive or otherwise.

> *"Achievements are sweet when I look back and*
> *reflect on how the seed of success was sown."*

I always say I am at my best when I am down or when people put me down because that is when I take risks. And when I take risks, I have nothing to lose but more to gain because of risks there are lessons of success to be learned. When people tell me 'you can't do' I tell myself

'I can do.' I know a lot of people who have not gone for their dreams because someone else had told them they could not do it. And whenever I have had conversations with these people, the first question I always ask them is, 'do you honestly believe you can't achieve just because you are in a different country?' I am often met with blank responses at this stage. Why?

Because unless you try, you can't tell yourself you can't. No one can tell you, '*you can't.*' Unfortunately, people who do not want us to progress will always tap into that weakness within us and convince us with uncertainty. In this short life of mine I have learned the hard way that people feed into our weaknesses, and because we are going through hard times and desperation, we believe them.

> *"Resilience is a part of every human's journey, the deeper the scars, the bigger the accomplishments."*

I don't always have mentors by my side because that would be handholding throughout life. Whenever I have had no mentors close by, I have trained myself to lie to myself that I can, even if I know that it is going to be a struggle to do what I want to do.

Why? I hear you ask. It's because I have to lie to myself to prove myself wrong afterward. When I lie to myself that I can't achieve a goal that is when I do everything possible to make sure that I aim for that goal. It is a technique I have practised for a year, and somehow it has so far worked.

FROM ORDINARY TO EXTRAORDINARY
"You don't have to be great to start, but you have to start to be great".
—Zig Ziglar.

My success is about exploiting opportunities. It did not come from just reading books or attending a particular school. I took up an Occupational Therapist course because the jobs I was applying for in the development sector all required for me to have at least 12 months' work experience in a developing country. I had tried to ask people for favours to help me break into the sector but without success.

I had tried to pursue the graduate scheme entry route, but I was also unsuccessful. Every route I tried to take, to penetrate the development sector has been unfruitful. The responses I received almost always sounded like this; *"thank you but you have been unsuccessful on this occasion, we will keep your details for future posts"* response.

I lost count of many applications I had put into different organisations. In the end, I felt defeated, but with that in mind, I had to quickly think of a solution which was going to get me a job so that I can start earning an income straight away.

A nursing degree came to mind, so I applied for a healthcare assistant job in a hospital so that I can see first-hand what was expected of me as a nurse. What I observed made me re-think the decision. I have immense respect for the medical professionals, nurses in particular, however, I had to think of whether I could do it as opposed to going into the profession just to earn a salary. I told myself that I was not getting any younger, I could not deal with long working hours and interrupted sleep patterns. I applauded those who were or are nurses and can do it; it is a true calling.

I then looked at physiotherapy. I was bad at biology and bones! I look at pursuing dietetics; the course was four years. That was a lifetime of studying, and my patience would not allow me to do a four-year course. I slapped myself across the face and had a moment of monologue sleepless nights. I was not going to be a carer forever. I could do better than that, I told myself. I had observed another profession on the ward; 'occupational therapists.' I was going to read about them and make inquiries. Someone mentioned to me that it was a profession that was difficult for 'black people to get into and succeed as it was dominated by white people.'

I looked at the entry criteria, and it had a bursary for it. That was enough for me to make a decision.

"I struck a deal with the impossible;
I was going to make it possible."

In my first year of the course, I struggled with every module to the point that I almost gave up. I made it to the first-year placement, and I had a mentor who told me that she was 'going to push me hard' because *'there is a great potential in you making it in life whether you become an occupational therapist or choose another career path after the course.'* All that she said was meaningless to me because I remember thinking, she made it difficult for me so that she can see if I was going to fail, and that I never wanted to see her again. Fast forward four years later after one year of practising as an occupational therapist, I have taken up a part-time role and set up my private business.

Her words reinforced all my other conversations with other mentors before her. That I can do whatever I want to do only if I manage to have a box always with me, then think outside that box. The one thing I have never been able to do even when talking with my mentors was to reflect. Reflecting on my abilities, what I can do, what I cannot do and what I can do to make things better.

ACCEPTING MENTORSHIP AND REJECTING DEFEAT

"You know, you do need mentors, but in the end,
you really just need to believe in yourself."
—Diana Ross

I wouldn't be where I am today without being ruthless, the way I have been in my life. Sometimes in life, one needs to be ruthless to progress. I have cut out negative people and ruthlessly selected the ones I think they will be positive role models. Ten years ago I was losing hope and faith. I was reliving the times, days when my family and friends were telling me that I was not going to be anything in life. I believed them.

The UK was not going to be my life or my destiny, and all hope of achieving the basics other than a basic vocational qualification and

CPD certificates was now becoming a reality. But I was handed a life-line, one that I was going to make the most of. I didn't have anyone to guide me when I started making life-changing decisions. However, I remembered everything I had been taught – when you aim for the flowers you reach for the fruit.

The most common mistakes we all make in life is fear and not being confident. The fear that we will fail or that we have failed once or twice before, so we are bound to fail again. We also tend to surround ourselves with people or individuals who may otherwise not be happy with any progress we make, be it progress with failure or progress with positive outcomes. Every investment carries some risk, and it is through those risks and failures that we learn in future investments. It does not help that those people are adding on to the risks.

Don't be scared to get rid.

STEPS OUT OF THE COMFORT ZONE
"Plant your tiny seeds and keep watering them every day. Soon, they'll grow."
—Israelmore Ayivor

I am always nervous when I am venturing into a new prospect. Sleepless nights and weird dreams combined. I live in a different country from the one I was born and grew up in. I am mostly surrounded by people who do not speak my mother tongue, and that is a given.

Oh hey, remember that resilience? We may be diverse and as culturally polarised as one can imagine, but there are some things we share in this diverse setting . . . resilience and ambitions.

I know about my dream and the end goal, but I am looking for someone to support me and facilitate me to shape the process. Someone who speaks the same language as I do. The language of resilience and ambition.

If you know you have people who do not want you to take risks then do not let them see your fears, because they will use your fears against you and your progression and your passion. Your mentor is the one who should know your fears, and they will mentor you in the right direction. Use your mentor, but don't abuse them. They are there to help and not to destroy you.

In my language, there is a saying which translates that 'where a king's son is having some wisdom imparted to him, you as a servant listen in.' We live in a world of possibilities, and it doesn't matter where you live in the world, the experiences are the same. Rich man versus poor man. White man versus black man. Woman versus man.

There are always barriers which stop us from progressing, but it is up to you to outsource an opportunity, a moment where you have to fight without getting exhausted and being left burnt out. We tap into opportunities every corner we turn, and those opportunities are the ones who will lead us to the prospects we aspire.

IN CONCLUSION

**'If you cannot see where you are going,
ask someone who has been there before.'**
—J. Loren Norris

Translate migration into a good thing. The best thing that has ever happened to you. There are mentors around us, and it may not be five, but there will be one who takes that leap of faith and sees the potential in you and gives you that belief and pushes to a possibility. You will end up speaking the same language. You will be comfortable in that adopted culture. You will break the glass ceiling of impossibilities. Take the chance. Because once you wash your hands, you should not let someone else cut the food for you.

The scars of resilience heal. You will be left with the blemishes to remind you of what pain felt or feels like. Think of a situation in your life where you have fallen to the ground, in other words, you have experienced a major setback, or you have been in the darkest of places. Then tell yourself that whatever you are going to do right now or next, you are not going to fall any lower than you did last time. You will always rise. So, do it. Dream big and go big. Wherever you are in the world, you are standing next to a resource; it's yours to use. It needs to be used, so use it.

"Whatever your dream is, don't let people tell you that you can't. You can!"

Clara C. Meierdierks

Born and raised in Nigeria, until I left Nigeria for Germany for further studies with the help of a girlfriend. I was born of late Mr. and Mrs. Patrick Uwazie, a family of seven, in Uwazie´s Compound in Ahiara, Imo State Nigeria. I am a Nurse/Midwife, Respiratory Care Practitioner (dip.), Qual-
ity manager (Cert.), BSc Health and Social Welfare, MSc Psychology holder, striving for more in the academic world. I am also a freelance, motivational writer, speaker and a blogger. Writing has helped me to fight some silent wars, ups, and downs, and have accompanied me in the darkest moments and days.

I am persevering, persistent, creative in writing. My motto is: "to be responsible, to use the lessons of yesterday to fix today, to be charitable, and provide confidence and encouragement to those I meet." I believe that we all are on a journey, and have different stories to tell.

Speaking/Seminar Topics: Health/Matters of Africa.

Books: Co-Author The Perfect Migrant, in the process of writing my first book which is due in 2019.

Contact Details:

Facebook: https://goo.gl/eW4Xtk

Phone: 004915231790068

Email: Hacla.meierdierks@gmail.com.

Chapter Seven

❧

MATERNAL BLISS DELAYED NOT DENIED

By Clara Chinyere Meierdierks
MY IVF JOURNEY

INTRODUCTION

As an African woman, children are very important and basic to our mental, social and psychological well-being. From an African woman and a nurse, I learned to be courageous and strong. I learnt never to give up, and because I knew deep down, I am a fighter.

"My IVF Journey" is a quest to have a baby through an unnatural way as we know, rather through an IVF, which is a procedure used in a high tech Laboratory to fertilise egg and sperm outside the body, and in turn after 2-3days depending on the clinic, is replanted in the womb as an embryo to develop in to full pregnancy.

Though my personal 'In Vitro Fertilisation (IVF)' struggle was hard, I was not at any time ready to give in to all the challenges of IVF. Once it worked, the pains of the journey were overtaken with joy.

This chapter is an accumulated work of many attempts, an effort that has caused me to want to quit or persist., An experience that I will not forget, a story that I think will be beneficial to many. Help others, tell their story. , I am telling the story of my perseverance. Whatever you are in to keep your dreams alive, remember you cannot achieve anything without faith and prayers. Believe in you, your hard work and powers of prayers, because prayer will strengthen your faith and lead you to success.

I am writing this story out of the experience I went through. Should you notice many repetitions, know that I am writing based on what I went through, the medical records, interactions between the many clinics and me etc., because most medical terms cannot be twisted.

"You do not write because you want to say something. You write because you have something to say"
—F.Scott Fitzgerald.

I write because I love writing.

I enjoy silence and use any chance to write. I have learned with time to work on my past through writing. I am on a journey like another person. I have stumbled, bruised and got hurt in the course of my journey. I have hurt people, and people have hurt me.

"This is my journey. I intend to talk about it."

I initially did not feel comfortable talking about my past. However, I think today I feel so comfortable talking about it, because I realise that one cannot run away from its past and, we all need our past to blink into our future.

However, many of us find it very hard to talk about painful past, especially we from African backgrounds. Either due to our beliefs or upbringings or the fears of what others will think of us.

I had had to deal with uncertainties, but today am glad, I have broken the ice, and I am here writing about this journey. This road, this journey with its challenges, is not an easy journey.

There is a huge world out there longing for help, encouragement, and word of support. These people scream for someone to stop and recognise that they are there and that they have burdens troubling them. Your story could empower, encourage and even turn their worlds around, don't feel shy to share your story. You could be helping someone in need. We live in a world that is engrossed with selfishness, which has no room to stop and feel concern for those with ailment and problems.

WHAT IS IVF (INVITRO FERTILISATION)?

(IVF) In-vitro Fertilisation a kind of assisted reproductive technology. It is said to be one of the options available and is medically recommended for infertility cases. This is with any biological procedure that is done outside the natural womb and is replanted after fertilisation outside the womb (source: Medical dictionary

It is seen as a medical wonder from God via medicine, to fulfil and complete families.

IVF per se is a process that involves removing a woman´s egg or eggs after stimulating a woman´s ovulatory process with hormonal drugs, at a 14th day cycle one Ova or many Ovum are removed (egg or eggs) from the woman´s ovaries and are fertilized, depending on how many viable eggs, they are allowed to be fertilised in a liquid in a laboratory, after which depending on the rules and ethics of the clinic and country the zygote/s are cultured for 2-3 days; some clinic can culture until five days (source: Medical encyclopaedia).

A JOURNEY THAT SEEMED SLOW

It is always our wish to end any journey well. Having all information concerning a journey does not always mean that the journey will end up well. When it does, we are so grateful to God. And when it turns out the other way round, we become sad, disappointed and even get discouraged. This is human nature and is not forbidden.

It is so easy to blame oneself or others when things don't seem to go our ways. But does this change any situation? No, it doesn't. IVF could be a long and exhausting journey, but worth going.

This is a journey of a struggle to have a baby through IVF. It is a real challenge, a hard journey I must confess, and not a bed of roses. I was not initially prepared to take up whatever challenges it has to offer.

This journey requires patience, faith, hope, inner strength and good people around you. Because this particular journey could take you to places that you could never have imagined to go. And it could pose a real challenge that could break or mar you, but yes you can, if you have faith.

In life, whatever you are going through, have gone through and will go through, always hope to find the right mindset, the strength, the right people and the right voice, to speak out when the time comes, as the time will always come. It may take years, but someday you will wake up to discover that you are ready. It happened to me; your case is not different.

After all, I found my voice, and I am going to encourage you through on this journey.

You are special, and you are strong, and you are just unique. -You are you, and you are embarking on this journey because you hope to get answers and solutions. So don't stop halfway: keep on trying until you excel. For, in life, those who win are those who in spite of all odds kept fighting for their dreams.

To those who have gone through this journey and to those who are yet to go through this journey, I hope my voice will join others in helping you deal with the ups and downs that accompany this journey. But believe me, we are all different, our lucks are not the same. Our way to success are equally not the same, but always be positive and don't allow those negative stories deter you from being a mom.

BEFORE THE JOURNEY

Before embarking on this journey, take a nice break, seek for a good adviser, and prepare as many questions as possible, because you will need them.

We all plan our lives to suit us. Some plan on marrying and getting pregnant and having children. Even though the Bible promises us that God will give us the desires of our heart if we believe and have faith in Him.

We are also told in the Bible that God will meet every one of our needs, not foolish ones without wisdom.

God knows better what we all need and meet us at His own time, but we must walk with faith.

STARTING A FAMILY

"Starting a family is very exciting and could sometimes turn out the other way."

When it does, please don't destroy yourself. Seek help, look out and find those who have been on this journey. You are not alone and will never be alone. You are not the first and will not be the last. There are so many on this journey, and you only need to search for them to give you the right coping mechanism. But please don't give up.

So many things in life are very uncertain, and that makes it somehow unpredictable in such a journey like IVF. I do not intend to dramatise anything to cloud against the moment or dampen your spirit. I have trailed on this path before, not once and not twice, am just one in a million that have gone through this lane, many times. I am writing from the point of an insider, who has known the agony of this journey, the pains and the isolation that goes with it. The doubts and the ups and downs.

Whatever uncertainty and hardships the IVF journey threw on my way, one thing I did not think of doing was quitting my dream, even after many storms in my life. There were moments of disappointments, criticisms, gossips and lot of failures. I found myself at some time surrounded by negative people who monitored and wanted only a positive result. And when otherwise the lion was let loose on me, I was left to carry all the blames.

My experience with my ex-relationships was not fair. Their motto was *"get a baby, or you are not worthy."* I held on to faith, to God. I nearly got drowned, but I did not lose my desire, for I knew that God would answer me one day.

EXPECTATIONS AFTER A UNION

We don't choose to fail in anything we decide or choose to do. It could be that things fail us along the way, which is certain to happen at times.

After the union of man and woman, especially after marriage, pregnancy is expected to follow society. When it fails to happen, again and again, worries set in, as it was with me. People start counting for you. The next move will mean making an appointment with your GP. When every result seemed okay, the next step will be a referral to an infertility clinic for further clarifications.

This goes with all sorts of anger and questions like why me?

One is willing as a woman to undergo any test because most African culture is careful with reality.

Initially, the visit may be only concentrated on the woman as usually the case. Even up to undergoing many gynaecological operations, if only that will help. Most women are victims.

So many women get pregnant every day in a natural way. At this thought, one begins to wonder why me. It is most disturbing when the doctor has done all test and kept on telling you; there was no problem, everything was okay. Until everything was not taking its natural place.

One feels so sad like the world is emptying on you. What follows is sorrow, hurt, anger, this is very normal, no reason to feel bad about it.

How long and how far with this bad feeling?

This is a question most couples asked themselves.

What is the next step, what other options are available?

Queries and search on the internet for every information on this topic follow.

THE FIRST VISIT

This visit may call for the initial experiments, that may include, maybe use of clomide, a tablet that stimulates ovulation. If nothing happens after, emotional tumult sets in, because the next step could mean, a total check of both the woman and the man. Things like HSG, the dye is injected into the uterine tubes, to check if there is any blockage.

If no blockage of tubes and if no fibroids or growths are detected anywhere, this could be a hindrance, if hormone levels are adequate. Any woman is ready at this point to do whatever.

If the test of the man indicates, poor sperm quality as it is always the case, low mortality, and morbidity, in the end, the doctor tells you both; you will need an IVF – which medically is used to overcome infertility.

At realising this, the world will first stand still and crumble for a while. Where I come from our culture does not make men responsible for any problem of infertility. Unfortunately, most men know even before they get into marriage what problem they have, but fail to disclose to their partners.

Naturally, a woman assumes all the blames until proven otherwise. Even so, men inwardly still deny the fact. Some go as far as seeking for other traditional ways that will exonerate them from facing the truth.

How can a man in an African contest be unproductive?

As they rightly describe women. As a woman in this society, you are bound to accept it is your fault, because men`s ego comes in question. Cry if you must but get ready for this journey that will give you answers and fulfilment and put you in doubts as well.

Initially, there is this denial that goes with this phase. No, it is not true, it can't be me, why me, and many whys follow until after a while. Seminars and talks on IVF will only at this point depress you. First, you won't want to identify yourself with the other couples with a similar problem. That is the self-denial at this point. This is okay, it is a healing process, as it gives one time to deal with the issues clouded in the head. Those who have gone through this, they surely know what I am talking about.

At this point, most clinics will offer as many tests as possible, with their checklists, and these cost money, time and emotion. It is very difficult to know which clinic offers the best reasonable care. Some will offer as many tests as possible. Be careful; you may think they are the best.

Our first attempt and all were with my ex-partner. One is desperate, naive and blind. They believe that *"yes"* one has a problem, and the fact that it could only fail at first attempt was far from real.

SOME OF THE TESTS AND PROCEDURES I UNDERWENT

Blood tests for FSH (Follicle stimulating hormone) LH (Luteinising hormone), TSH, the doctor will tell you it is usually done on the 3rd day of the cycle). If all goes well, the doctor will inform the couple of the next move, which is stimulation.

Progesterone

Prolactin is also tested, If FSH and LH are not okay, the clinic treats and correct.

HSG which is the x-ray of the uterus, to check the tubes, is done on the 8th day of the menstrual cycle.

Day 10 and 11 are normally for checking the state of the ovarian state and thickness.

HSG (Diagnostic Hysteroscopy).

Pelvic Ultrasound.

What I realised later from one of the doctors was always to ask for the test's results,

HIV, hepatitis, VDRL, immune testing, TB,

Bundle of papers to read and sign.

Questions concerning the reproductive history, medical histories.

Clomiphene citrate challenge test that is what the doctors call it.

Antimüllerian hormone (AHM)

Imagine seeing, and reading about all these for the first time; I was overwhelmed and imagine what war my mind fought!

I wanted to scream, was my thought, because I was so tired and did not know how to think. I wanted to pretend, but could not. I wanted to behave as if nothing happened but could not, forcing myself to be composed was not at the moment in mind. It was like waking up with nowhere to get hope.

In this broken heart, broken spirit, with tears of raindrops. That was my kind of tears.

This is what it looks like when we do not understand why things happen, even when we understand, the pain is there. After all, understanding why cannot take away the pains of a broken woman with a broken dream. What was left was to scream for the reasons why everything did not work.

DIFFICULT MOMENTS

It was so difficult to make the pretence. Although, I made efforts to look fine and appear strong. With these heavyweights, thrown in and out, ready to drag me down. The soul was broken, the mouth could not hold its own pains. So afraid inside, because I was helpless, broken and lost. So, the rain was let to drop, and I cried my soul to tiredness.

> *"They will say you are weak when you cry, broken heart, but you are the strongest when you decide not to hold your tears back."*

Tears of a broken woman - Most women cry from the outside to reduce pains. Most men don't and call it bravery.

When pregnancy does not come naturally after few months, IVF is seen as an option as it was in my case.

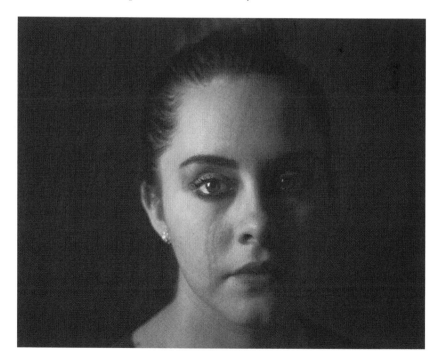

Crying sometimes is the only thing left when we have no option. It makes us feel better sometimes but cannot take the hollow away from us. Crying cannot make all right but can refresh our thoughts. Heaven knows that this kind of tears is like raindrops. We all on this journey have had raindrops on our eyes. I tried to release my pains and the realities that go with IVF.

WHY ME?

I was not ashamed. I cried so hard that my throat was hurt, but I did not mind, that was truly painful. Deep within everyone in this situation is a need to weep alone, to stay alone for a while and sort out issues, and to ask "Why me."

What I could not help at every moment was take the pains away,
The pain sited in,
No one could help,
When you look at,
Or spoke to this face,
In this agony,
Tears would flow,
Sobs, uncontrollable.
Tears that only hope, faith
And God can heal.
These are tears of agony,
Tears of a broken woman,
Sink and lost.

WHAT TO EXPECT

You will hear jargons and terms from the doctors, with every arm full of papers, to read, digest and sign. Who fixes this brokenness! Of my thoughts, the fears of many tests and procedures, the needles, injections, and swallowing of pills, the countless visits they intruding into one's privacy, that reduces one to an object, the fear of what if, and the many ifs?

Will you pretend not to mind? That is a war, a battle, that will create the desire not to let the broken moment, the uncertainties, the doubts, and the many hopes, expectations, of our dreams, pass us by.

IVF "real" or "illusion"?

Many questions like "*why me?*" fill the mind and the mind begins to wonder where to get answers. The journey becomes an illusion, clouded with fears.

IVF is the only option left.

A medium growth is then transferred to woman's uterus with all hopes of having a successful pregnancy.

It is medically advisable that every couple in this journey requires three attempts to realise this dream. Some are lucky at first attempt.

I began this journey since 2007. However, all the five failed attempts were with my ex-relationship. Every trial began with a high positive spirit; it was only in 2015 that I was able to smile.

We complied and did everything demanded of us as at then. Fortunately, at the first attempt, I did not need any increase in hormone, and all seemed to favour us. We were happy at the turn of events.

There were many things I don't know, but quite a few I do. I know you can't be lost if you know where you are going to. I know that life is full of positive and negative things. All I know is that there is a fighter in me, and with God, I will battle until I get an answer. I know if not today then tomorrow. Life will always pose a challenge on our journey. Remember you have God, Fight back. When you lose never go back to the beginning, sometimes, we can start again, with hope and faith"

The first time during this journey follows your feelings of relief because one is getting somewhere and knows that something is being done. When conclusions are made, in whichever cycle to begin, scans are carried out to check the uterine level; this follows next level, stimulation with injections, and tablets. Injections could be painful and hard, because it is not a matter of one shot, many shots, but bearable shots, because of the expectations.

Next will be another scan to check the progress of the ovaries; this is the point that determines whether to increase or decrease the number of injections or no injections at all or if the follicles are not doing well, could lead to the termination of this phase to be started all over again. If successful, a date is set for the next phase.

THE 'D' DAY

The day of extraction will come, the whole procedure is done under narcosis and when you wake up, the tension that follows, asking yourself, "are the eggs healthy"? Because sometimes extraction of eggs does not mean all are ok, the embryologist tells you the number of extracted eggs.

The journey begins. You will be told to go home and wait for a confirmation call that will either tell you what next to do or to say sorry, the eggs were unable to fertilise or so . . . You find yourself waiting and getting panicky at any phone call of any sort. You get agitated, lose appetite and have mood swings. Finally, finally, the call you have been waiting for comes and a voice on the line, that has good or bad news, speaks.

A CRUCIAL WAITING

This is another crucial stage of your waiting. News that will take you to another level of your journey, news that will shine hopes or dampen your spirit and make you want to quit.

At this moment you don't want to engage in any long talk. All you want to be told, all you want to hear is; "congratulations we were able to fertilise your eggs," or "we are sorry it did not work-followed.

You are expected at the clinic at so and so time, for the implantation., or the other way round.

On This Day

Back to the clinic on the transfer day, scared, but keep praying for things to go well. The implantation process will last about 30 minutes, following which I am expected to lie down for another 30 to 60 minutes. I felt I did all right. I followed all the instructions and was exceptionally very careful.

Now, for the first time, the two-day embryo was implanted. There were hope, fear, and leaps of joy. Some people may decide to take leave, but the embryologist told me to go about my normal life and try to avoid any stress of all kinds.

The uncertainties in the first attempt made me take 15 days leave from work. On the 15th day, the test was carried out to ascertain the success or failure of the IVF.

The nurse said Negative. First I felt it was not my result, and wanted another test, which she asked me to repeat the next day . . .

Those were endless waiting's; I felt feels like exploding in my thoughts, my head, I lost my appetite.

The repeated test did not change anything. My hopes were dashed; my heart was broken again.

JOURNEY NUMBER SIX

Six months after recovered from the shock, I went back to my gynaecologist who had time to talk with me. She encouraged me and gave me referral paper that will take me through to another journey. I had been through these processes five times in my previous relationship. You can't imagine the agony, the pain of feeling isolated, of seeing most of my mates, friends and even my junior ones getting easily and naturally pregnant. Of course, the question lingered in my mind. "Why me?"

I made a more thorough search on the internet; asked friends; sought advice, and even went to Spain all on a quest for answers.

Unfortunately, none of the clinics could give me the positive answers I was yearning for, the chance of having a baby, being complete and finally being happy. Despite all these negative answers, I knew deep down me, there was this fighter in me, who was not ready to give in to all these negative results.

I then opted for adoption which my then partner agreed and later disagreed due to the pressure. Incidentally, the relationship could not stand the pressure and then broken down. I then suffered the separation and all the pain and sadness that went with it. Another load of pain and sadness was added on top of what I was already carrying.

I was lost. I lost all hopes. I thought my world was ending and my dreams were shattered. In short, although I gave up the idea of getting married I never gave up the burning desire to be a mother.

After about six months of suffering from the separation, I ran into my husband in a supermarket, and that was it.

We told our stories, he heard my story and was ready to take another journey with me.

Six months after we met he proposed marriage and six months later we got married legally in church. The joy that follows could not be described. God´s own time.

We decided to take another IVF trip, of course at our own cost, because insurance was not going to assist once you are 40 years old.

At this time, I was so knowledgeable about the IVF process. I undertook long research; I found an incredible recommendation about a clinic in Nigeria. I received so much support from my family, my few friends Vivian Timothy, Sister Gloria and my husband, Hagen. A year after we were married went through the IVF again.

This time it worked . . . finally, **I had a positive result.** Thank God, I achieved my goal. Praise the Lord!

LESSONS AND ADVICE

To all those who are intending to embark on this journey and those who have made more trips.

I have had my journeys, and that is why I am taking time to let you know that you are not alone, and will never be alone on this journey. Show yourself love instead of bitterness, don't be too hard on yourself or your partner. Pray, seek for your strength and look for answers at the appropriate places. Although one cannot give you a hundred percent answer or a shortcut to this journey.

Everyone's journey is not the same, be positive and don't be discouraged in your journey.

Avoid situations that are not encouraging especially negative people; they can be additional stress and not necessarily helpful in starting off this IVF journey.

The IVF journey is not an easy journey, but what journey is easy in life? No matter what, dare to embark on the journey; it is worthwhile. Make it your journey and be patient. Many couples who were interviewed described this journey as one of the most unpredictable, devastating, heart-aching journey ever. But it can be made, with so many positive results along the way.

> ### *If you don't try, you will not know what it means to fail.*

Don't forget life itself is a risk, and risk is there to be taken. You have to try, and not get scared. After all, you will never know if you don't try. You will realise how much stronger you are in the face of, perhaps, one the most challenging journey you will never take in your life. You will learn to never quit in the face of any challenge.

Of course, I see it as a challenge, for whatever reasons, it was not in God's plans to challenge any couple with this. No woman is born barren and for the fact that you have to go this journey does not make you any different from any other woman.

It may sound hard, but you are different, you may not end with heartbreak. You may be one of the few lucky ones that make it in one trip. Bare in your mind, in case if you want to take this journey. Go with faith, for, in the end, it is only but the faith that will take you a long way.

IVF is very safe according to medical experts and is nothing to be ashamed of. Once you are left with this option, make sure your doctor explains everything to you and your husband.

Research and inquire after clinics with success rates. Plan your programmes, which include your work, take a holiday. Discuss cost and be very sure. Have an open mind, the journey can be exciting and at the same time nerve breaking.

Be well informed at any stage, ask for every test done on you, and prepare as many questions as possible.

After many trips that failed, one is bound to have luck even if it means once. Most couples have broken up because of the failure of the woman to conceive. Naturally, cases of divorce, bullying of the woman from the partner and even in-laws have been reported.

This is the time people will come up with different accusations. Some may even say oh, she was wayward. Even the man who medically is responsible for this will allow you to be frustrated.

Sometimes and even all the time, most things happen for a reason. Separation may be God's ways of telling you. My child, I have something better for you. I suffered separation when this journey was not yielding positive results.

After I got separated from my ex-partner, I met my husband, my love, my hope and my God sent him to me. Who took me for what I am and was ready to journey with me?

WE DID THE IVF AND TO GOD BE THE GLORY

"Good news is something the soul longs always to have."

16th Nov 2015, a very special day that gave me my fulfilment. A long way to success. It does not matter how long it took me to get to this day. I saw this day, behold this day as the phone call that generally would murmur something in the past, like Sorry Mrs. It was negative,

But guess what?

This day the 16th gave me a soothing, smiling happy voice that did not hesitate to tell me the good news.

"Mrs. Meierdierks ... Congratulations! The result is positive."

Imagine what I did, at first, I did not realise it was me she spoke with on the phone. When I did I busted out in tears, tears of joy, tears of relief and what I did after hanging off was to call my husband at work.

My love we made it, 'Chiagorolam,' God has vindicated me.

GOOD NEWS - A DAY TO REMEMBER

Good news is good for the body, the whole system.

How will it look like when all our days are filled up with good news?

The heart is relaxed, the body is at peace, and the system functions well, and the mind finds its peace and work goes on.

What can I say and what can I offer you, my dear Lord, from this day I promised to dance and celebrate God. It is also on this day I made up my mind to speak generally on this journey, for the lots of women broken and soaked in tears.

God said it is over. He answered me and so shall it also be unto all of you my great women seeking to conceive. When I started this journey, the days were as if it will never come to an end. I worked with my calendar and knew even every colour in every month. I was getting angry and so worried. Sometimes I try to calm myself down. My husband was calmer. That's men for you.

I stopped counting the days and allowed the days to count for me. Jesus is the answer, and Jesus answered me.

On this day, a day that has gone into my good record, a day I have set aside as a special day.

The ultimate day that measured where I stand, where I should be and what God intended for me. At times of challenge and controversy, it takes a lot of courage, to go through the pains, the loss, the dejection, and the empty feelings.

Life is not all about success; it is also about failures, loss, and disappointments. These life's challenges are things we are bound to encounter in our life's journeys. They are there, and we can't simply avoid them. So be ready to deal with obstacles when they come to your ways.

It does not help so much to look constantly at the past. Otherwise, you will miss the next train taking you to your future.

I can't tell you that it was an easy journey. Many of you that have walked on this lane may know what I am talking about. It is not all about pains, the desire, the waiting, and the counting of days. It is all about you and what happens; when all efforts were not rewarded?

What do you do?

Cry your heart out?

Resign or give up hopes?

Many of us have ways of dealing with issues. I dealt with my empty and lonely days through writing. I write and write, because I know there are so many out there itching to hear other people's stories. Instead of breaking my head and wondering what went wrong, I learned to do it this way.

The thought that always goes with each attempt is, oh it would be great if this turn out positive.

There were impossible odds that could hold me back from success. I tried to overcome these failures, disappointments, each time I am stricken down. I refused to let the fear of defeat accompany me; Of course, I had my moments when I let my emotions flow.

It was so natural for me those days to worry, to break down and cry; it was something very natural to cry to God and tell Him my stories, despite Him knowing it all.

No one has a special talent to cope during these moments. Only God's will is the best. Pray for confidence and believe that God can do anything He wills. This is very important to success. If you don't have the strength, energy, and determination, to believe in yourself, continue praying God, continue at every given opportunity, pray and pray.

It does not mean that you were never meant to succeed. I will urge you to keep on trying as long as you want to succeed until you succeed.

"Try, sooner or later, those who win are those who have accepted the challenges of failure and have learned to try one more time."
—Jeff G.

When you are down, you are not finished, because God is not finished with you, why should you then give yourself up, when God is there to help?

Anything that delays you from achieving whatever plans you set for yourself can only be a blessing. Think back and let the truth of the 18th-century spiritual writer Jean-Pierre de Caussade, sink in:

> *"Whatever happens to you in a day, a month, a year,*
> *for good or bad, is an expression of God's will."*

Instead of cursing your luck, banging your head, or rolling your eyes in frustrations, see it positively.

As I learned:

"when you get into a tight place, and everything goes against you, till it appears you could not hang on a minute longer, never give up then, for that is the place and time that the will turn"
—Harriet Becher Stone.

God answered me, He will also answer you at His right time, but don't give up, for

"MATERNAL BLISS: Could only be delayed and not denied.

Lucy Oyubo

Lucy is the CEO and Founder of Hakuna Matata Language and Cultural Exchange based in Basel, Switzerland. Her school was founded in 2010 with the help of the Gründungszentrum Crescenda, an organisation that promotes female immigrant entrepreneurship in Basel. She is also  a qualified Interpreter and a translator. She Interprets and translates Swahili, English, and German in different Institutions and court.

Lucy was born and raised in Busia, Kenya. After completing her Bachelor of Education (B. ED) studies at Kenyatta University in Nairobi, Kenya, where she majored in Swahili and PRS (Philosophy of Religious Studies. She moved to Switzerland in 1999. She opened a school called the "Lakeside English Centre" where she is proud to have taught English and Swahili to thousands of students.

In 2015, her school, Hakuna Matata Language and Cultural Exchange were awarded the Company of the Year Award by the African Woman in Europe (AWE) organisation.

Lucy was also featured in a book written by Crescenda; It is entitled "Das Crescenda-Modell" and it is about female entrepreneurship.

Area of Expertise: Teaching, Interpreting and Translating

Books include; (1). Das Crescenda-Modell, (2) The Perfect Migrant, and (3) Celebrating Diversity.

Company: Hakuna Matata Language and Cultural Exchange

Contact Details:

LinkedIn: https://www.linkedin.com/in/lucy-oyubo-b4993434/

Facebook: LOyubo

Phone: +41(0)76 578 4555

Email: lylum22@yahoo.com

Websites: www.suaheli-lernen.ch

Chapter Eight

❦

HUMBLE BEGINNINGS AND CAREFREE VERVE!

By Lucy Oyubo

EARLY CHILDHOOD

"Hakuna Matata, take it easy, no matter what!"

—My slogan.

I was born in Busia, Kenya, a small town on the border of Kenya and Uganda, near Lake Victoria. After getting married to my Ex-Husband Mr. Osterwalder, a Swiss, I moved to join him in Switzerland where I have lived for 18 years.

We are six in my family. I have three brothers and two sisters. I am the, "Only lost sheep" meaning, I am the only one in the diaspora. All my siblings are in Kenya.

I am very proud of my parents. My dad Karoli Oyubo Nakhwanga was a Criminal Investigation Officer but retired very early. My mom, Mathilda Ong'eti Oyubo, was left to be the primary breadwinner for a long time. She was, and still is a strong woman, even at the age of 77. My dad died in 2007.

As a child, I really had big buttocks, and I was nicknamed, 'matako makubwa,' meaning the 'big buttocked one,' and I was fat too with big cheeks. I hated it and kept fighting my elder brothers back because they bullied me very much. I am the fourth born and the first girl, so I was always expected to set a good example for my sisters. Although we afforded to have house helps, my siblings and I still chipped in to do the house chores, and sometimes everyone looked at me for a solution as the eldest daughter, when there were issues to be solved.

We had one bike for the whole family. It was always quite difficult for us girls to ride it because our brothers would not let us. But being strong-minded I fought with my brothers until I started cycling a massive bike at the age of six years. I remember always running to pick up the bike whenever our parents sent us to the shops.

Since my parents couldn't afford to buy bikes for each one of us, we all went to school on foot. My younger sisters and I went to a girl school called Busia Girls Primary School, and the boys went to Bulanda Primary School. Both schools were like 20 minutes walk from our home. I am so proud of the fact that we didn't have electricity, did our homework using lanterns during our primary education yet we all worked hard and performed well in our exams.

I loved going to school a lot. I feel humbled that I was able to go to school up to the University level. Our parents were very proud of all of us. They both encouraged us to work hard. We were brought up trilingual, speaking Swahili and Luhya, my mother tongue, and English in school.

I started having the passion for languages when I was still very young. I used to admire my teachers very much. Teaching had been my dream job as a child, and I am so happy that my dream was fulfilled.

My mom keeps reminding me how at the age of four, I had started singing that I was going to marry any man who treated me well and would make me happy, be it a Chinese, Indian, white, yellow, black, it didn't matter. And that I was going to travel to a far land and leave everybody behind. My mom saw my dream being fulfilled.

That dream came true when I married a Swiss man Martin and moved to Switzerland with him.

HOW I MET MARTIN AND THE AUSTRALIAN DREAM

I met Martin when I was teaching in Masai land at Olkejuado after my University education as a single girl for almost ten years. My parents had given up on me ever getting married and having kids. I then married him and left Kenya. My love for people from all walks of life seems to have started when I was still very young. I am always asked if I do not miss my family very much. The answer is; *"I would be glad to visit them four times a year if I could afford it."* It was a bit difficult to communicate with them when I moved to Switzerland, but now we have mobile phones, Skype, and WhatsApp. I can call any time I miss any family member.

I was lucky to fulfil my dream of leaving my country, Kenya. When did it happen? I met Martin during my second visit to Switzerland, to attend my friend's wedding, Gabi, and Fabio Fiore, way back in 1996. Gabi's father, Francis De Haas, whom I had met in Kenya, working on a Kenyan-Swiss project, was kind enough, to buy me a ticket and invited me to attend his daughter's wedding ceremony. He is the reason I am in Switzerland; thus, I know I shall never be able to thank him enough.

Martin who is now my Ex-husband was a close friend of Jolanda, who was a close friend of Gabi and Fabio. I was lucky to visit them twice here in Switzerland while still living in Kenya. They also visited me twice in Kenya. So, we were pretty close. Martin and I didn't contact each other for a while after my second visit to Switzerland because we had both lost each other's contact.

Then through the help of Jolanda, who had introduced us to each other during my second visit to Switzerland, we found each other again. Dated for a few years, visiting each other until we decided to get married. Gabi and Fabio flew to Kenya to be our best maid and bridegroom at our wedding. By the time we were getting married, I had been accepted to do a master's degree in Public Health at Wollongong University near Sydney in Australia.

I have excellent friends in Adelaide, Australia, Sue and Peter Lambert, who had even visited me in Kenya, and I was quite looking forward to studying in their beautiful country. I have visited Australia several times, and it is the only country that I would happily move to if there was an opportunity. If all would have gone according to our plans, our wish was to settle in Australia after my studies. We then got married, but unluckily enough, after our marriage, I was denied the visa although my polite and lovely Father-in-law had even footed part of my University fees.

What I couldn't do while in Kenya was to prove to the Embassy that I had enough money in my account to take care of myself while in Australia, and that is how my dream to study, move and live in

Australia went down the drain. Martin was also willing to join me in the future, because he was ready for an adventure like me, and this saddened us a lot.

I had visited Switzerland and stayed with Martin in his small but beautiful town called Romanshorn, situated in the northwestern part of Switzerland for three months after our marriage. It was before I was denied the visa. We agreed that I visit for a while to see how and where my husband lived then. I had only visited the country twice but like a tourist.

I was here both times during summer and was able to visit other neighbouring countries like Austria, (Schladming where I learned how to ski), Italy (Naples which I adored because I felt very much at home, due to the easy-going behaviour of the people as opposed to here) and Germany. But this time around, I visited in winter.

I didn't like the weather and found the Swiss people quite boring. I hardly met people on the streets who spoke English. It was quite frustrating because I could not speak a word of German. We were both very excited that we were not going to settle down here. During these three months, Martin made sure I was not bored.

He bought me a special three-month tourist ticket called, 'General Abonnement' which, enabled me to travel all around the country. I left the house almost every morning with him going to work and came back at night. He was always looking forward to listening to my adventures. It was an amazing experience. There are times when I came home and said, *"I was in Martigny today, or in Locarno, or Brig, La Chaux de Fonds"* and sometimes he would go like, *"where the hell is that?"*

The challenge came when I called him at midnight to seek his advice while stuck at, for instance, Mustair or Interlaken Ost after missing the last train and sometimes he was short of good advice. Naturally, I got to know the country much better than him as a Swiss native. He was very proud of my courage. Especially the fact that I couldn't speak any of the three main languages in Switzerland, but that was not a problem for me. Some ladies would have shied away from travelling on their own; I found it fun.

Another reason that made me want to leave Switzerland without looking back and thought I wouldn't have regretted it was because of the behaviour of Martin's landlady. Martin was living in an apartment below the landlady and his family. He was the only tenant. Martin's landlady had been very friendly to him until I arrived.

In the beginning, the landlady was quite pleasant to me because she could speak a bit of English and was happy to practice it with me. The landlady could never face me and point at the things that I did which angered her.

For instance, she could talk to me very well in the morning. Later on, in the evening when Martin comes back home he is told; *"Ihre Frau hat heute den ganzen Tag Bush Musik gespielt"* which translates; *"Your wife was playing bush music the whole day today."*

I remember getting astounded also when she said at one time, *"Sie kocht mit Knoblauch und es stinkt überall"* meaning *"She cooks with garlic thus the entire place stinks."*

Isn't that amazing?

I can see those who live in diaspora and have maybe experienced the same thing smiling.

It was also a taboo to laugh or talk loudly. Martin would also tell me to reduce my voice. He could say shhhhhh at me. I would be like;

"What? Schatzi! Can't we do what we want to in our homes?"

He said to me when he answered; *"We have rules here. No noise after 22:00."*

You should not even flash a toilet at night to avoid disturbing your neighbour's sleep. Or you are not allowed to do laundry after 22:00, or on Sundays and during holidays. This is also forbidden even if you have no immediate neighbours.

The washing room was never cleaned to the standard expected by the landlady. We kept having wrangles here and there. But always complained about me through Martin and I have never understood up to now why she couldn't face me. To be honest, I was happy to go back home after three months, thinking I would never be back to Switzerland again. Little did I know this was the country that I would come back to and have to follow all these regulations and even more.

After being denied the visa, we contemplated on whether we should stay in Kenya or move to Switzerland. Martin was unsure if I was going to cope with the weather and his own culture. He was quite ready to join me in Kajiado, Kenya, where I was teaching. But because it would have been difficult for him to get a job there, we decided otherwise. We decided to come back to Switzerland, stay for a few years, work, save and invest before we could move back to Kenya after some years.

I followed Martin in April 2000 after resigning from my school and came back to Switzerland ready to face life here and do the best I could to integrate. The first move we made was to shift house. We were pretty lucky to find our own little house with a big compound. You can imagine how happy I was. I made friends pretty fast, at the German school, my neighbours, or my students. We had parties after parties and felt so much at home. Here, as you can see in the photo, I am with Martin having fun in our garden in the summer, feeling happy.

We had a lovely time together. We gave each other space. He didn't like dancing, but he let me go. He didn't come with me to do activities that I liked, like swimming, hiking, or even going to the gym. But I met friends who like these sorts of activities, and I joined in. I quickly learned ice-skating, because we lived near an ice skating rink. I quickly learned skiing as well and kept travelling almost every year with some friends to ski in Schladming, Austria, where I made so many friends until now. I just read the other day that the famous Kenyan skier Sabrina Wanjiru Simader was brought up in Schladming and learned how to ski there. I would like to imagine she was still a toddler at that time though.

Martin loved travelling. So, we travelled quite a lot together. We both enjoyed every bit of our travels. We avoided buying a car and going out for expensive dinners and saved money instead to travel. We have been to all continents, from Australia to Africa, North and South America to Canada. We are lucky to have friends in all continents. Mostly, we went to places where we knew people and were able to mingle with the natives and learn the cultures. We both enjoyed that very much.

Fatefully, our marriage started going to 'the dogs' in 2005. Who knows? Maybe the marriage could have been saved had Martin had agreed to us seeing a therapist. Despite my efforts, he insisted that he didn't see the need. Eventually, I gave up. We separated from each other for two years and had an easy and mutual divorce later. I then moved to Basel while he moved to Locarno in Switzerland.

Even after our divorce, we are still very good friends. I appreciate the fact that even after our divorce, I am still able to continue travelling on my own and visiting friends on all my trips.

MY LOVE FOR SPORTS

I grew up loving all kinds of sport.

I liked cycling a lot, because Busia-Kenya, my hometown is a town of bicycles.

The number of bicycles (bodaboda) at the time I was growing up was remarkable compared to other cities in Kenya. The situation has changed now; it is tuk-tuk.

My passion for bikes made me spend the whole salary that I received after my first month at work on a speed bike which cost about 80 Euros at that time. I still remember how proud I was of myself. The local people at Kajiado, which was the town next to the school I was teaching called Olkejuado High School, did not know my name. But if one visited the town even at present and asked some of them if they remember 'Mwalimu wa bike' meaning 'the bike teacher', they will smile and say yes. And my students too could look through the window and go like, 'Mwalimu wa bike ana come,' or the bike teacher is coming. I must admit I had a fun experience as a young teacher in Maasai land. I miss every moment of it.

For example; I once met a former student of mine in Zürich. I had forgotten about my biking experience back at home because it had been a while. The boy was so excited and couldn't stop calling me; *Mwalimu wa bike* and narrating to a whole group of friends about my speed bike, how fascinated his schoolmates were about me. The fact that all these aspects were coming from my student's point of view was amazing because I would never have known some of the things he mentioned in my life. I felt very proud of myself to listen and laugh about it.

My school's library in Kenya caught fire and got destroyed in 2004. A co-teacher, Anne, an American Peace-Corps worker and I, decided to cycle from our school to Nairobi for a good cause. We wanted to raise money and buy new books. For some reasons, Anne couldn't make it.

I ended up cycling by myself, and you can see me arriving in Nairobi on my bike on the photo. Although we managed to buy some books, unfortunately, not all the people who pledged honoured their promises and even as I am writing now, there are those who have never paid their dues. I apparently, still have the list with me.

I enjoy climbing mountains too. I am proud to have been blessed to climb Mt. Kilimanjaro 3 times while working as an instructor at the Mountain School. The school, I am not sure if it still exists was at the foot of Mt. Kilimanjaro in a small Maasai town called Oloitoktok in Kenya.

I worked with a lovely group of instructors during my school holidays whereby we disciplined disobedient students from different schools by doing tough, physical drills and outdoor activities with them and writing reports about improvements in their behaviours. We guided cadets and some tourist to climb Mount Kilimanjaro.

I have also been at the peak of our beloved Mount Kenya many times especially during my duty as an instructor. I loved it so much, such that I begged Martin to climb Mount Kenya for our honeymoon. He couldn't believe his ears, because he had never climbed any mountain.

We travelled to Nanyuki, a town at the slopes of the mountain, organised guides, bought some food, rented a tent and took off. We slept in a tent the first night and in a hut the second one. We both had an amazing experience on the first night of sleeping in the tent.

Imagine sleeping in the same tent with a partner, it is cold, dark and wet outside and one of you has eaten lots of beans for dinner, and none of you can go out for fresh air! I survived though. We kept making jokes about this experience for a long time after that. The joke was, if we didn't part ways then, we were going to stick together for better or for worse forever.

Unfortunately, Martin caught the mountain sickness on the last day when we needed to climb the last lap to the peak and walk all the way down to Naro Moru . My dreams were fulfilled half-way because we had to hike back to Nanyuki. I was quite happy that he didn't say no from the beginning.

I am happy that I can continue exercising my passion here in Switzerland. I have been lucky to be able to hike many mountains like Mt. Pilatus, The Säntis, The Rigi, The Churfürsten.

During our travels, I had the opportunity to climb the sacred Rock Uluru or Ayers Rock some years back. It is forbidden to do it now. I also experienced the beauty of Cape Town, South Africa when I climbed the uncountable stairs of the Table Mountains to reach the peak of this adorable mountain.

I love skiing, snow hiking, ice-skating among others. As this is not a very common occurrence for my fellow Kenyans. Some fellows claim that I am trying to behave like a 'Mzungu' (a white person). I do believe in the saying, 'when you go to Rome, do what the Romans do.' A lot of people wonder when I talk about having a passion for doing these typical Mzungu/white-people sports, asking me if I was born here. Being who I am, started way back home. I lived near a river, thus the passion of swimming, while teaching in Kajiado. I climbed Mt. Kenya several times and started cycling as a small girl while in Kenya.

If there had been a possibility to ski on top of Mt. Kilimanjaro maybe I would have learned how to ski as well. Nobody believes me when I tell them my age and my answer is usually, because of my love for the sport.

I guess it's unfair to put everyone in the same basket. Everywhere you go, you will find people with exceptional characters. I have lived in Switzerland for so long and have met Swiss people who have never climbed any mountains, never skied, because it is an expensive sport, or some are not interested, and some do not even own a bicycle or like cycling. Martin and I used to joke with each other, about the fact that he was the black Kenyan man, and I was the Mzungu Swiss lady. He didn't like skiing, hiking, swimming, going to the gym. So I did lots of these activities with friends.

I am sure most of you black skinned people have been asked, just like me, if you do not freeze so much in your residential countries in Europe because you come from warm countries. I have been asked this question many times.

I do not believe in some people freezing more than others because of where they come from. We have some Europeans running away from their cold countries to move to warmer countries because they freeze here, just like some of us who live here from warm areas. I am not sure if any blacks or Asians are running away from their own countries because they want to come and enjoy the winter in Europe or America. When it gets too hot in their countries, they also suffer, just like those tourists who come from cold countries suffer in the heat.

We all have the same blood, and all freeze our asses off when walking around in the cold in the wrong clothes. It's a question of what you wear in the cold. Sometimes when I am asked if I do freeze a lot here in Switzerland by someone who is wearing a very thick coat, I laugh. I say yes and then request them to hand me their warm coat so that they can walk around without it to confirm if the level of freezing they experience is different from mine. If so, then I guess Europeans could be walking around in bikinis during winter. This is my own opinion; you are allowed to give yours.

Another point that I would like to make is that I have been asked this question many times'

"When do you intend to go back to your country of origin?" I am sure many of you who are single are asked the same question. To me, the question sounds to me like,

"When are you planning to leave our country and go back to where you belong?"

If there is anyone out there, who gets irritated like me, here is a suitable response that I always give, especially if I realise the question is out of malice. I do ask them how many black people they have seen in the old people's homes around Switzerland! Their answer will, of course, be none. Then I tease them, *"I am not going anywhere because I want to wait and go to the old people's home with you."* Try it, and you will see how humble and apologetic they will get, because honestly, most Swiss people, young and old, hate to imagine they will get old one day, and they distaste even the idea of thinking they will land in an old people's home one day.

I grew up near a small river where we, as kids, used to go swimming almost every day. Swimming is another sport that many of us coloured people do not do because we are afraid of the water.

I was fortunate to move to Romanshorn, after my marriage with Martin, which is a Lakeside town. We lived a few minutes from the lake. I continued with my swimming passion and could sometimes swim in the mornings and evenings. I love water so much. I keep joking, that my death will happen in water. I remember how Martin used to react when I went on holiday with him and disappeared into the deep waters sometimes for over an hour.

Whenever I got back, he could say,

"Hey Schatzi/sweetheart," do you have any idea how helpless I would be if a shark or something attacked you?

He could be restless keeping his eyes on me and only felt relieved when I came out of the water. That was so cute of him. He didn't very much like swimming and couldn't stay long in the water. Something that I have noticed that many Europeans do when on holiday. They wake up in the morning in their hotels, have breakfast, go to the beach to lie on the decks, apply lots of sunscreen on their bodies, and roast their skins in the sun like white maize back in Kenya. Some of them do not even touch the water, or if they do, it is only for a few minutes.

I am so happy that I do have dark skin. I could not trade it for anything. It is appalling when I see our young black girls bleaching themselves to look white, yet the white people are roasting their skin in solariums and in the sun to become brown. Life is a riddle. I am so grateful to God for my dark skin and for being who I am.

Then I was again lucky to move to Basel a few years later, which is a town on the famous Rhine river. I adore my summers in Basel. Swimming down the River during the hot summer days makes Basel my most favourite city in Switzerland. It is a special thing because one can buy a floating bag, called *"Wicklefish."*

Wear a bikini and put your clothes inside the floating bag and seal it. Then hold it, jump into the water and let the stream push you down the river. I do not like holding the bag, so I usually look for friends to go swimming with them so that they can carry my clothes for me. It is an amazing experience which I would urge those traveling to Basel during summer to try by all means.

I taught my students Karate, and it was amazing seeing them getting excited to be taught karate by a lady. I did the Karate course while at Kenyatta University in Kenya, and my objective was, to defend myself. There were many uncouth boys and men around, and I felt very strong to defend myself sometimes when someone touched my buttocks or my breasts in public as they always did and still do to young defenseless girls.

I must admit I had some street fights and was happy to surprise those men who thought all of the ladies were cowards. After each fight, I told myself I was helping those who were helpless in a way because these men would think twice before they harassed any other ladies.

I have lived in Switzerland for a long time. But honestly speaking, I am still very bad at keeping time. My punctuality is only perfect like a Swiss when I have an appointment to interpret in Courts, the Prosecutor's Office, hospitals, and schools. Or when I have an appointment with a doctor. One always has to be careful because if you do not appear, or arrive late; you will be charged 50 francs which is the equivalent to about 5000 Kenyan Shillings (KSH). Paying such money for nothing can be very painful. If you are reading this and live in Switzerland, I guess you are smiling because you have been a victim in your life.

I am sure the doctors here earn a lot of money from migrants because most of us have a problem with keeping time. Or some even forget the appointment. If you are not lucky to have a doctor who sends reminders, then you could pay for it the hard way. I do have a lot of fun with my Swiss students especially when they are late, I tell them, *"Listen, I am the Swiss Lucy now, and you are the African Mary."* We laugh about it.

There are those who have been told by Swiss people when they are late that, "Wir sind hier in der Schweiz," meaning, "We are in Switzerland here." I usually quote to them my friends who always come late. I guess at times we have to be tolerant of one another.

The other thing I struggle with is following the traffic rules. Having been used to drive in the streets of Nairobi for many years, it has been almost impossible to adhere to Swiss rules. I am always being fined. Either I have parked badly, I have forgotten to display or adjust the blue parking card, or the worst of all, I have over-speeded. There is a lot of portable radars in my city of Basel; such that one does not know where and when they are placed. I am always a victim of them. The reason being, I do not concentrate on checking the speed limit but drive. I do sometimes wish that I was living in Germany because one can be warned about the whereabouts of the portable radars on the radio. Doing this is considered a crime in Switzerland.

I am contemplating on getting rid of my car because owning a car in this country is an expensive thing. The transport network is very good, so I guess it is time to stop working to pay fine bills, enriching our Basel Municipality. I could endlessly talk about other facts about me, but I guess that would fill up a book. I hope you can learn from my mistakes and be a better person.

I cherish the fact that I live in this country because I can embrace both the Swiss and the Kenyan cultures which makes me feel so lucky.

TORN BETWEEN THE TWO CULTURES

Living in Switzerland for 18 years has changed me a lot. I am a naturalised Swiss. Before Kenya accepted dual citizenship, I decided to keep my Kenyan passport just as a consolation although I knew that I needed to declare it. Unfortunately, when my dad passed away, and I used it, to go to Kenya, it was confiscated, and the immigration officer, of course, wanted 'Kitu kidogo' a bribe. I refused to bribe him after which he said, *"Go back to where you belong."* I was so hurt that this words still ring in my head.

When I was in Switzerland, I knew very well that I am only a Swiss-by-paper, like they say, because my colour shows otherwise.

When I am in Kenya, some of my fellow countrymen on the streets mistake me for a black American or a Jamaican.

Even right now when I go to Kenya, my fellow country people tell me straight on my face that I am not and feel like a Kenyan anymore. I used to feel hurt, but not anymore.

No one has unfortunately ever explained to me the reason they think I am a foreigner. Even when I dress up shabbily and go to the market, I am given higher prices like a "Mzungu" a white person?

I have challenged my kinsmen several times to give me the reason as to why they think I do not belong to them but have never got an appropriate answer.

I hear stuff like, there is something about the way you talk and the way you walk. Even those I speak Swahili to claim I could have learned it from a Tanzanian or abroad.

When I was in Kenya in December 2016, a lady told me there is some weird politeness in you, the way you talk softly and showing thankfulness. I just laughed, because those people who know me properly here wouldn't buy this joke, I guess. But sleeping over this point, I remembered that I had kept greeting people when I went into a shop and saying bye.

It is a behaviour you have to get used to. In Switzerland, when you enter a shop, you will be greeted and when you leave you to have to say bye. The shopkeeper may not necessarily be quite friendly to you, but rest assured of a bye when you leave.

When I lived in Kenya, and my white friends visited me, I am the one who used to go and negotiate prices for them so that they could pay less and save some money. Believe me; this is exactly what I do now. It is my turn, in my own country, to look for a fellow countryman to buy stuff for me, because I will pay more if I went alone. This mainly happens when you want to buy some curio stuff. It breaks my heart.

Most people have also experienced the same thing in other countries. I remember when I visited Jamaica with Martin some years back and decided to travel around on the same bus with the natives from Kingston town to Port Antonio. Martin was the only white man on the bus. The conductor shamelessly demanded double fare from both of us.

We had seen how much the natives had paid, so I demanded to know why we were paying double. He bluntly told us on our face, that, "the white man has money, he deserves paying more, and because you are together with him, you also have to pay like him." We were left speechless.

Walking around Jamaica with Martin was scary. In Kingston Town, we kept being warned to be careful. The drama started right at the airport. We had not booked a hotel in advance, as we were coming from Havana, Cuba, expecting to find one when we arrive spontaneously. They could not let us in at the airport until they were sure we were safe. They booked us a room in a private home and demanded we take a taxi. By the time we were leaving, we had encountered so much that we could easily write a book about our two weeks experience.

I usually compare my dear Kenyan people to the Germans. They are both more straightforward and will tell you off on your face, unlike our neighbours in Tanzania or Uganda. The good thing is that we are all used to this behaviour. When the Tanzanians visit Kenya, they get a shock of their lives when they listen to how rude we sound, speaking to each other. Tanzanians could easily be compared to the Swiss people who are kind, polite and with less guts, a typical example here is my landlady. I always compare the straightforward-ness of Kenyans to the Germans. The Germans and Kenyans do not sound rude to their people, especially when they order something in the restaurant/bar, but when they visit their neighbouring countries, they sound super rude.

A Kenyan will order for a drink in a bar and say;

"Wewe weita, leta beer mbili baridi hapa" which in English translates;

"You, waiter, bring two cold beers here" pay attention to the direct translation which may sound wrong to an English native, but stay with me, I am trying to drive a point.

A German person would say *"Ich kriege ein Bier bitte."* In English, "Bring me a beer please."

I would compare the politeness of Tanzanian with one of the Swiss people here because in Tanzania they say, *"Naomba bia baridi tafadhali,"* which means literally, I beg for a cold beer." While the Swiss would say, *"Ich hätte gerne ein Bier,"* meaning "I would like to have a beer."

During my travels, I have been able to observe different people, with different cultures, and different behaviours and this is what I find very interesting. Without diversity, life would be so boring.

I must admit that some years back, I got so confused that sometimes I did not know who I was. I feel better now because I had to undergo some rebirth, a ritual, to accept the fact that I will never be a Kenyan again and I can never be a Swiss. Martin witnessed this fight in me. I remember him having so much sympathy and even advising me after our divorce to return to my country. It took me longer to find myself.

I feel much better now and have learned to accept myself and make the best out of the fact that I am here, and ready to make the best out of my life until the time I will decide to return to my motherland. I do not want to go to an old people's home here.

Have you ever been in a similar dilemma? The only way forward to accept who you are, make the best out of the place you now live knowing you only live once and there is no need to spend a lot of time finding yourself.

MY TAKE ON THE MIGRANT LIFE

1. Learn languages that are spoken wherever you live. This will open ways for you, no matter what!
2. I believe there is no problem that cannot be solved. Do not give up easily. Keep fighting. And you will be surprised.
3. We should always give a win-win situation. You feel very ululated when you realise that whatever situation you find yourself in, with your partner, or friend, or job, that you are both happy.

4. You will always feel blessed if you do good to others. Always be ready to forgive.

5. Avoid eating junk food. I do. I have been asked many times how comes I look so young at 50. My answer is usually, eating well, thinking positively, I do a lot of sports, and finally, I have no partner because sometimes they can stress you up unless you are lucky. And this makes me feel so good.

6. Think positively and do what makes you feel right. Avoid doing stuff that makes you feel like shit at the end. I learned this the hard way.

7. Appreciate what you have. No need to be jealous of others. This will not take you anywhere.

8. Dancing, Dancing and again Dancing, is my therapy. If you can't make it to disco, dance in your living room, kitchen or bedroom. It is the best therapy ever.

Lwiza Mulenga

Lwiza is passionate about Anthropology and International Development and in charitable work and volunteering. She is an influencer in the charity sector to support women and children. She holds a BA Hons in Anthropology and International Development at the University of East London.

Lwiza first volunteered in Cambodia for three months in the province of Battambang during her gap year.

Born in Zambia in 1994 who is the first born of two. Lwiza's father passed in 2003, and soon after her mother sought a job in England. In 2006 Lwiza's mother moved her and brother to England, West Sussex.

Lwiza enjoys spending time with her family (mum - Justinah and brother - Romeo). From whom she gets the most inspiration and courage from to do what she loves from.

Lwiza also enjoys exploring different countries, reading books, writing blogs and real estate acquisition.

Contact Details:

LinkedIn: linkedin.com/in/lwiza-mulenga-ba5546121

Phone: +447984287093

Email: lwiza94@gmail.com

Chapter Nine

☙

SITUATIONS DICTATE OUR LEARNING

By Lwiza Mulenga

INTRODUCTION

Arriving in a new country as a young person can have its challenges. It can also give one opportunity that other people only dream of. As a child migrant, moving to the United Kingdom was both happy and sad. I had just lost my dad who was a significant person in my life. If you have ever lost someone special in your life, you know what that feels like. The situation was made easier when my mum Justinah told my brother and me that the three of us were to move to the UK. I was very excited about this news. I envisioned myself sitting with my friends and having a laugh. The other side of me was a little bit scared, scared of the unknown I guess.

What if I don't like it?

What about school?

Will I miss Friends? Yes, my friends, I am going to miss them. I will also miss my aunties, I thought.

Alas, it was not my decision, I had to move with my mum. She knew best; she had our interest at heart. She wanted a better life for us all.

Soon I started mentally preparing myself to fly!

HOW I LEARNED TO READ AND WRITE DIFFERENTLY

On November 28th, 2006, I moved to England at the age of 12 with my mother and my brother. My mum had been offered a job as a nursing assistant in England, so my brother and I had to move with her. This was going to be my first Christmas in England and I most definitely expected snow as I had seen in films I watch back home in Zambia.

Can you imagine my shock when I woke up on Christmas morning and there was no snow, but a lot of rain?

Shocking! I was somewhat disappointed. Nonetheless, my first Christmas in England was amazing. The streets decorated with beautiful lights.

'Christmas trees everywhere and a lot of chocolate to munch on.'

We spent our first Christmas with Aunty Bonde and her family, who made the experience unforgettable. Christmas was short-lived, and I was to start School in January.

I was excited to start school, ready to make some friends and be a regular kid. However, nothing could have prepared me for my first day in a new school in a new country. As I entered my form room and was introduced by our form tutor, my nerves grew every second. A room is full of girls who all knew each other from the previous year. In the UK, secondary education starts in year seven, and grades change every September, whereas, in Zambia secondary school starts in year eight and grades change every January. This meant I had missed out on 15 months of British secondary school education.

I sat with three girls, still nervous. I reintroduced myself to them, to break the ice and start a conversation. They all looked at each other as if I had spoken some foreign language, then one of them spoke, and I was even more confused.

"I believed we were both speaking English, but we did not understand each other."

There was such a big difference in our accents. This continued in class; I found myself not understanding what was being taught.

I had already missed a year and three months of secondary education, and then I was struggling to understand what people were saying. Imagine how lost you would feel if you found yourself in such a situation? Your confidence is killed. Moving from the top of my class in Zambia to now not even comprehending what I was being taught, was crushing for a 12-year-old.

One day my Aunty B came to pick me up from school. She noticed I wasn't the cheery girl she was used to seeing. She asked what the problem was. It was such a relief to explain to her what I was experiencing, opening to her changed my life; we talked for while which helped me feel better about myself. She told me she understood that me moving to a different country could be difficult. She advised me to start reading anything, I liked. This would improve my English and expose me to a whole new vocabulary of words. Little did she know this would encourage me to write better.

For all you, millennials, you know the Twilight frenzy that encompassed our lives since 2005. Team Edward or Team Jacob? I was introduced to the Twilight book series in 2009. It's safe to say I was a super fan because eventually, I started writing. I was so obsessed with Twilight that when I finished reading the books, I joined a fan fiction website Twilight Fan Fiction. I read most of the stories.

When I was not satisfied with what others had written, I started writing my own stories.

And that my dear friends, is how I started writing. So, I have three lessons to share with you:

> **"If you don't like the story, write your own"**
> **—Chinua Achebe.**

1. **Write Your Own Story**

   The above quote is one of my favourite quotes and when I was 15 years old, that is exactly what I did. If you don't like the story, you can write your own story, do not settle for someone else's story if you are not satisfied with where the writer left off.

2. **Strength comes from Struggle.**

   You learn from your most significant struggles. If you are in any new situation and you are struggling, find someone to talk to. A lot of adults are willing to listen; you are not alone. Communicating with others who can't speak a language will help them build their confidence and increase your language skills too, so it's a win, win situation.

3. **Most change is hard.**

   Whether good or bad. However, it is what you do with the change that has happened to you. That is what will define you as a person. Writing is a great way of coping with situations so right away!

READY TO TAKE A LEAP

Are you stuck in your comfort zone, or maybe you are at that point in your life where you don't know what you want to do with your life?

We all have dreams; it doesn't matter where in the world you are. We all have the ideal life we want to lead. For me, I have always wanted to be a millionaire. I have dreamed that I will retire at age 30 and live in a good neighbourhood.

The reality is different. When I was young, my mum did everything for me, even when I was at university. My mum always sorted out my bills. My view of the reality of what people do to be successful was not something I had even considered as a young person.

When I completed University, I struggled to find what I wanted to do with my life. I was so worried about how my life was going to turn out. I love helping people, and I like different cultures. I also like working with women and children.

So I decided to raise funds to go as a volunteer, anywhere in the world to work with women and children.

Before I start anything, I am always confused and all over the place. But once I make a decision and start, it's like the dark tunnel. I am scared of entering and then becomes bright without me even lighting it. Once I make a decision, the universe starts to respond to me. But coming to that decision is not always easy.

My experience in Cambodia taught me a lot of new experiences. The food was different, the people are very friendly, in a way it reminded me of being back home in Zambia. The three months I spent there made me grow up. I was able to look after people who were younger than me, which made me feel quite grown up. When I came back to the UK, I was ready to face the grown-up world. I turned to my mum and my aunties who are my mentors for help and advice, Before long I realised that I had to make my journey.

I started working in a job I didn't like. I told myself, "I will work here for exactly 12 months" then I will be out.

That is exactly what I did. After 12 months, I started a business venture, which didn't also work out very well.

Soon I realised that life is not always as it seems. My dream of being a millionaire needed more work than I was able to fit it at the time. My dream is still alive, but I now have a more realistic view of life. One day it will happen.

> **I would encourage you to set high goals.**
> **Set goals that, when you set them, you think**
> **they're impossible. But then every day you can**
> **work towards them, and anything is possible,**
> **so keep working hard and follow your dreams.**
> **—Katie Ledecky**

I always turn to people that inspire me. I am very comfortable asking questions. As of late, there have been **stories from people like Mwape Chibwe,** A Zambian woman who has immersed herself into the water sanitation industry, as she follows her passion for making sure there is clean water in Zambia. Her journey of leaping into a man's world of Water Engineering with only the belief that she could make a difference in the world and leave a legacy. Her sheer determination always brings my head back to what I want to achieve. She said something that stuck in my mind. That the first time she approached a mining industry to get her first contract, she was discouraged by someone she knew who said she couldn't do it.

"It is impossible you are a woman and this a male-dominated business . . . you won't be able to last."

She did not let the fear of not having enough finances or the stereotype stop her. She also was ready to accept that situations didn't happen because of her gender.

"If it did not happen for her it was not because she was a female or any other reasons. It was because it was not meant to be."

A lot of people including me, have a hard time accepting such situations. But in whatever you do this is the most important counsel to keep in your head.

Often, we start working on our dreams, but we lose the zeal and motivation to keep going. We forget WHY we started. We get discouraged on the way, mainly when we hit some bumps in the road. I decided to leave the rat race at the age of 21 because I believed another day, hour, minute, or second, doing what I did not believe would advance my own goals.

So, what is it that you have wanted to do?

What is that thing you know you should be doing but are worried about your finances or what others think?

Maybe start your own Business, travel the world or simply just become a better you. Keep that dream alive and take the leap. Start working towards it every day.

HERE ARE MY THREE LESSONS, ON TAKING A LEAP

1. Remember every day you put into someone's dream, is a day taken away from your personal goals. Think and act today. Do not procrastinate.
2. Act without fear of rejection and feel confident, strong-minded and energised, and people will never reject you.
3. Ask yourself, are you living to work or working to live your own life?

Rod Khleif

Rod is a passionate real estate investor who has personally owned and managed over 2000 apartments and homes. As one of the USA's top real estate, business, and peak performance luminaries, Rod has also built over 22 businesses in his 40-year business career several which have been worth tens of millions of dollars.

He is a real estate investor and host of top YouTube and iTunes podcast 'The Lifetime Cash Flow through Real Estate.' Rod also runs various courses in multifamily property investment and business success.

A compelling rags-to-riches-to-rags-to-riches story, Rod Khleif soared from humble beginnings as a young, impoverished Dutch immigrant to incredible success. Rod's experience involves both remarkable triumphs and spectacular failures, which he affectionately calls "seminars." Rod brings incredible authenticity and insight to his approach to business, success, and life. Rod believes in family first, he is based in Sarasota, the USA with his wife Tiffany and two children, but works have clients from around the globe.

Books Include: (1) How to Create Cash Flow Through Multifamily Properties, (2) 29 Fatal Mistakes Many Apartment Buyers Make, (3) How to Find Off–Market Deals in a Hot Market,

Area of Expertise include: (1) Multifamily Real Estate Investment (2) High-Performance Coaching (3) Business success

Contact Details:

Website: https://rodkhleif.com

Podcast: https://www.youtube.com/channel/UCbb357-0yQw0kd NelWKrSkA

Facebook: https://www.facebook.com/groups/229962354193594/

Chapter Ten

☙

DUTCH MIGRANT TO MILLIONAIRE PROPERTY INVESTOR

By Rod Khleif

Interviewed by Amina Chitembo

There is no passion to be found playing small—in settling
for a life that is less than the one you are capable of living.

—Nelson Mandela

WHAT THREE THINGS CAN YOU
SHARE ABOUT YOURSELF?

I immigrated to the United States of America when I was six. And I guess this is one of the things that I would mention. We didn't have much; we couldn't buy new clothes. We lived in Denver Colorado. My mom had to babysit so that we could have money to eat. We wore second-hand clothes and drank powdered milk because that's all we could afford and expired bread.

From that, you know watching my mom, her hard work and being inspired by her, I ended up finding over two thousand houses that I rented out, multiple apartments, buildings and built up a network worth of over 50 million U.S. dollars.

"Everything begins with a high level of
self-consciousness and a dream."

I'm proud of that very much; this is one thing. I've owned about eighteen businesses; some of them were successes, and others were spectacular failures. I will tell you there's a punchline to that first point about building fifty million dollars network, that was in 2006. I owned a hundred houses here in Florida, and I think anybody reading knows what happened in 2007 and 2008. The recession hit.

"So, I had my largest seminar (failure) ever, you know.
I lost eight hundred houses about 50 million".

What was interesting was, my multifamily portfolio did just fine, which is the reason that you know I wrote my book about my family investment because I don't want people to experience the same thing. I believe that in the United States we're headed for a contraction pretty soon and if people are focused on the value of their asset versus the cash flow they can get in trouble.

I did get my clock cleaned now I'm back financially, and there are lessons to learn from that experience. I'm helping other people from that experience. So that would be the second thing. I would say, it ingrained into me, that the psychology is to accept failure or the loss, then take action and move forward.

To recover from losing fifty million dollars and not want to destroy my building, that's all in the mindset because as you know, 80 percent of your success in anything is psychology and only 20 percent the actual information. So luckily, I had that framework to get me through 2009 and to give me back to the success that I enjoy today.

The third thing, I have incredible work ethics, but I never went to college. I barely graduated from High School. My 18 years old son who's about to go to college uses this against me; he's like *"you didn't go."* Well, I work hard to be where I am today. But I think that one of the other things I am proud of today is the fact that I am very well read. I've got this huge library, and I feel like I'm probably even better read than most college graduates.

So, I mean I don't discourage anyone, particularly people of my son's age from going to college, but I will say that there are many ways of learning. And for me it is all about believing in yourself, having some or developing your confidence, pushing through the fear and being okay with taking action.

HOW DID THE IDEA FOR YOUR BUSINESS COME ABOUT?

"We are a country where people of all backgrounds, all nations of origin, all languages, all religions, all races, can make a home. America was built by immigrants".
—Hillary Clinton.

That's a funny story actually when I was 14 years old. Back to my mother again, she bought a house across the street for, I think, it was around thirty thousand U.S. dollars and when I graduated from high school that house was worth in the fifty's. *And so just by the passage of time, she made twenty thousand dollars.*

Although I hate math and I flunked basic math in school, I was able to do that calculation. When I was 18, I was already a real estate broker, which is the highest-level designation for selling real estate in the US. If you could do it back then through education rather than experience, now you got that by experience. I didn't know what I was doing; my first two years in the business didn't give me any business that made my mother proud of.

In my third year after you know, drinking through a fire hose studying the business, networking and learning the business, and the most important piece I think is that study turned into competence, and that competence turned into confidence, you know, and I made a lot of money my third year. Then I never looked back and started buying properties and houses in Denver. I ended up buying five hundred houses.

Then, I bought Two hundred houses in Memphis, Tennessee, and also bought over Thirteen to Fourteen hundred houses in Florida.

HOW DID YOU GET CAPITAL FOR YOUR GOT FIVE HUNDRED PROPERTIES?

You mean how did I come up with the ability to secure capital? Sure well, you know, money is just a thought. Money is, in my opinion, knowledge, and education. I bought five hundred houses with partners. I had them for all the money, and I managed them for half (you know how somebody bought out all my partners, but they put up the money to buy the house).

In that case, it was me, it was my competence, my confidence and my ability to influence that got me those first five hundred houses and so I think that's the case, and really, it comes right back to psychology. I had to have psychology necessary to be true when I was communicating with potential partners and investors and have the ability to influence them.

ARE YOU SAYING YOU DON'T NEED TO HAVE A BIG BAG OF MONEY TO START A BUSINESS?

You do not; You need to be willing to learn and study and focus on the psychology as well. I think I care if I do two sections a week in one of them, you know, it is just an interview with an expert in the family business. (this sentence is a bit unclear)

And the second one I'll call the psychology of success. This talks about everything from determining your goals, the responsibility to bear and the confidence. Have in mind you're going into this; it doesn't matter whether you like it or not is not only a coming from, you can still get to where you want to go. And if you can get through any obstacles that pop up in your way.

I think because anyone that wants to get in the business of any sort is going to have setbacks, they're going to have never built things that come up. So, it's critical they have clearly defined goals, clearly defined reasons. So that you know they don't lose focus and lose sight of the school where no inevitable setbacks occur.

WHAT BARRIERS OR FEARS HAVE YOU HAD TO OVERCOME IN YOUR BUSINESS LIFE?

The biggest one, of course, was 2008, the loss of the business through the recession. That was the biggest setback of my life. I thought I didn't even know that the United States baby boomers that were getting older and getting older would ensure that Florida was recession proof. Well, I got that seminar in Florida; it was one of the hardest hit states. But you know getting half the fact that everything I worked for was evaporated and I had this very challenging Obstacle, and again if I haven't been blessed to have been around Tony Robbins frankly, it could have been devastating for me and prevented me from pushing forward.

But I'm stronger than I was back then I went and rebuilt, but it was a tough time and very painful time. It was a lot of soul-searching, getting back to keep focused on what I want versus what I don't want.

Anyone should focus on what you want not the things that you don't want, as it was so easy as negative media environment to just focus on the negative but you get what you focus on, and frankly it doesn't matter how big it is, if you want to have enough you should be willing to work to get it. There's nothing you can't do. You know, if you focus on what's wrong you will manage and fight.

That's a good lesson to learn, and that's a very good one. So, regarding the struggles.

WHAT MOTIVATES YOU?

"Your desire to succeed should be stronger than your fear of failure."

What motivates me?

I write my goals almost every day. I'm looking at my computer monitor as we're speaking here, and I have things written.

So, you know what motivates me and what I teach people when I coach.

You must clearly define your goals. You must write down a paragraph for each of the goals; I would recommend that you don't just write positive life. I recommend also writing negative reasons why. I don't want to feel like a failure; I don't want to feel like I let my family down. And I realise that's challenging, but people will do more to avoid pain and try o forget about it, but I advocate acknowledging the negatives as this will help you move away from it.

The first few pictures I have are gratitude pictures. Because everything comes from the place of gratitude. That I've had pictures of things that I want, and how to have them. The watches I wanted, On it.

Every day I've got a little because I focus on what I want to like the runaway that I did well, the secret and the movies about the law of traction, yet it works. It works, and you know I realize some analytical people may see this article and think that's not true, but I can show you I have manifested everything I want in my life including my wife! And let me show you one of the Next is Radio.

You have to put the things in front of you so that your mind sees them. You get pictures of your goals and keep them in your forefront, and your mind will recognize opportunities to get you closer to your goals, so you know that's my advice as it relates to getting through obstacles. Because if you know your outcomes, you know why it's a must.

If you can see an obstacle, you'll change your approach. And you know if you had another offer you change your approach again. You may have met your goal from multiple angles, and don't get it if you have a powerful enough reason why. So, you know I like to tell the story when I got my broker's license really to call or not and that was a four-door car because I was told real estate (all real percent) never had a four-door car to take people around. Look at probably the ugliest man you ever see you know I was lucky enough to drive my fight for the Corvette.

I put the picture of that Corvette *on the bike for the sun visor,* and through two years I got it. You know I could give examples. I always wanted a house on the beach. On as it relates to that story, goals are very important, but you have to be very sure when you reach your goal that you're about to set up the goal beyond that. The Good Book says without a vision the people perish, and you need a vision for the future.

I was floating in my pool in this magnificent house, with the beach on one side, and the baby on the other side. Being a multimillionaire, and I said I did see everything I've ever wanted, but I got very depressed. And why I was depressed, you know, this was back in 2000, and when I look back on it, two things happened.

One was what I just mentioned. I choose for, and I didn't have any other quote set up, and I so needed a vision for the future. Number two is because I wasn't fulfilled and there's a big difference between success and fulfilment, you know. I know billionaires that are very successful, but they're not fulfilled. Tony Robbins called the finest of achievement versus the AH.

As Tony Robbins says, *"Success without fulfilment is the ultimate failure."*

So, I have a contribution to charity with my wife. You may be interested in success, but you need to make sure you incorporate giving back into your lives because that's where true happiness comes from.

WHAT OTHER THINGS DO YOU DO?

I started a foundation back in 2000, and you know Tony Robbins speaks to millions of families a year, and I decided to pick five families. So, for Thanksgiving we got food, and we deliver it. The Second or Third family changed my life. I walked up to this depression house, you know, this woman came out, she saw all the food and started crying, and then her five children came out, and they saw all the food and started crying, and I share the price, and I was hooked.

So, the next year, I fed fifty families, the next year a hundred families, and then two hundred families and then four hundred families a year and then in two thousand six hundred eighty families. I was making contributions but to south Sarasota, I formed a foundation called Tiny Hands, and we have now over fifty thousand children. I've given thousands of backpacks, building schools, supplies to local school children, so they have basic school supplies.

We've given thousands of teddy bears to police departments for the officers to put in their vehicles when they counter a child that may have traumatic experiences and that's been my greatest sure fulfilment. But I will tell you, that it doesn't require anything of that magnitude.

You can just decide to smile at everybody you see today, and you know, or to do something for someone. It doesn't require big grand gestures. But, if you're interested in success do not lose sight of the fact that you're really in this world to be happy.

All that success is really beautiful in your mind to become happy, and you can become happy by giving love and happiness truly.

WHAT ADVICE WOULD YOU GIVE TO
SOMEONE STARTING THIS JOURNEY TODAY?

Sigmund Freud said; *"words have magical power. They can bring either the greatest happiness, or the deepest despair, they can transfer knowledge from a teacher to a student, and words enable the speaker to sway his audience and dictate their decisions."*

Words are capable of arousing the strongest emotions and prompting people to take action. To be a success in life and business, you have to be a great communicator with the people you're trying to influence.

Throughout history, our greatest leaders have utilized the power of words to stir us emotionally, to rally us behind their causes, and to change the course of history. Using the right words, in the right sequence can create love.

In our lives . . . . we can create success in our business, and respect from our peers. Buddha said words have the power to both destroy and heal . . . . When words are true and kind, they can change our world. Words contain power. That power can be positive or negative. It's important to be careful with the words that you speak because once they're spoken, they can't be forgotten, they can only be forgiven. Words have started and stopped wars. They've built people up, and they've torn people down. They've instilled people with courage and have also filled them with fear.

Words when combined properly have the power to do incredible good or unspeakable evil. There are over a half million words in the English language according to Compton's encyclopedia, but the average person only uses about 2000 of those words regularly. Less than half of 1%. And the words we use most frequently, for most people, it's only about 2 to 300 words.

Also . . . . We all know that we can use words to express how we feel to other people . . . . . but you may not realize that the words we say to ourselves on a regular basis create our reality. By changing the language, you habitually use when speaking to yourself and others, you literally can change your experience of the world. The words can cause you to change how you feel, what you think about . . . and how you experience life.

Take for example if you go through a situation that causes you upset, there's a huge difference between saying you're furious about what happened. . . . versus saying you're just annoyed. Those two words create entirely different emotions and affect your body and your mind completely differently.

"Be whoever you want to be regardless of your race, educational attainment or where you find yourself in the world."

—Amina Chitembo

Acknowledgements

The Diverse Cultures Publishing aims to produce easy to read, books and other publications that will empower and encourage productivity and high-performance, personal and professional development for all people regardless of race, creed, colour, sexual orientation or religion.

As a dyslexic who did not have many opportunities to show my creativity and love for writing in a world where people's view of perfection is sometimes so narrow that people like myself are excluded. Once I discovered my condition in adulthood, I decided to take action and start writing. However, I was faced with the issue that no big publishing company will look at me twice if I walked into their door with a less than perfect book and pitch. So, I decided to start my own publishing company.

I wanted to help people like me to find their voice and passion for writing.

I am very thankful that the authors in this book believed in me and my proposition, and herein we launch our first co-authored book published by Diverse Cultures Publishing. I would love to say a very special thank you to all the authors of this book 'The Perfect Migrant':

Introduction: Amina Chitembo
Chapter One: Beatrice Hofmann
Chapter2 Two: Charity Ngugi-Latz
Chapter Three: Laura Tinzoh
Chapter Four: Gianluca Zanini
Chapter Five: Angelinah Boniface
Chapter Six: Pamela Mahaka
Chapter Seven: Clara Meierdierks

These people have shared their stories so that you can enjoy having an insight into their lives.

I hope you find it useful and empowering. Furthermore, I hope it helps towards reaching your highest level of achievement. To handle all your goals with the purpose and dynamism of a 'sports person'!

I would like to pay special gratitude and thanks a woman to took the difficulties of her journey and turned it into an organisation that is helping a lot of women find their strength, the lady is Joy Zenz and her organisation African Women in Europe has been helping African women to be shown in a positive light across Europe. Her work and passion are empowering to many migrant women. It is passion and vision that makes the world a better place.

I would also like to say thanks to all my associates, my family and all the professional who helped make this book a reality.

I would also love to say a massive thank you to you the reader for supporting our work.

Further Reading

Life is fascinating. Reading about other people's journeys give us a level of growth that no other actions can give us. As we end this book, I want to draw your attention to my favourite books from Migrants that I have enjoyed over the last year. In no particular order enjoy the list below:

1. And Still I Rise Paperback, by Dr Maya Angelou (Author)
2. Diversity & Inclusion: The Big Six Formula for Success, by D. A. Abrams
3. Migrant Architects of the NHS: South Asian Doctors and the Reinvention of British General Practice (1940s-1980s) (Social Histories of Medicine), by Julian Simpson (Author)
4. Migrant Women: Crossing Boundaries and Changing Identities (Cross-cultural Perspectives on Women) by Gina Buijs (Editor)
5. Migrant, Refugee, Smuggler, Saviour by Peter Tinti and Tuesday Reitano.
6. Millionaire Migrants: Trans-Pacific Life Lines by David Ley
7. One World Anthology: A Global Anthology of Short Stories, by Chimamanda Ngozi Adichie (Author), Jhumpa Lahiri (Author), Vanessa Gebbie
8. The Migrants, by Salma A Siddiqui
9. Who are Refugees and Migrants? What Makes People Leave their Homes? And Other Big Questions, by Michael Rosen (Author), Annemarie Young (Author)
10. Why I'm No Longer Talking to White People About Race, by Reni Eddo-Lodge (Author)

About Diverse Cultures Publishing

Founded in February 2017, Diverse Cultures Publishing is an award-winning subsidiary of Diverse Cultures Ltd based in the UK, with a worldwide reach. We are an ambitious type of independent publishers whose aim is to promote authors who would struggle to compete for traditional publishers. We offer opportunities for non-authors to become authors. We believe anyone can write and become a published author provided they receive the right type of help.

Our services are personalised and individualised, clients enjoy a service that is tailored to their needs. The founder Amina Chitembo, a creative dyslexic was for many years told she could not write or read, decided to defy the odds and challenge the norm by becoming a writer and later founding Diverse Cultures Publishing.

We work with a diverse range of people, and we are ethnically sensitive. We believe that language is varied and there is no pigeonholed 'English' in the 21st century.

Our vision is to see everyone who has been told they can't write, to defy the odds and become a published author. We work with the imperfectly perfect!

We know that not everyone can write a whole book and market it on their own. We also love the fact that co-authoring enables you to reach more readers and teach more people than you would have otherwise done on your own.

We provide opportunities to individuals to write their own books, to publish their completed manuscripts. We also enable people to co-author short stories in our advertised titles. We work with books in the following categories:

1. Leadership Series
2. Transformation Series
3. Diversity Series.
4. Autobiographies

CAN WE HELP YOU?

We are passionate about people becoming a published author. If you are looking for a friendly publishing company, we will be happy to help. We will help you to co-author chapters in personal and professional development books. Facilitating you sharing your knowledge and teaching what you know to help other people through the books and our International Authors and Speaker Conference.

You will also leave a legacy for future generations. Cool, right?

Come and talk to us, we are here to serve you!

We encourage and support people who want to pass on their knowledge and raise their profile, to become published authors.

Why not be one of them?

Below is are some of our titles:

1. Black Men in Denial? Challenging Social Beliefs on Black Men and Prostate Cancer, by Ali Abdoul – June 2018
2. Celebrating Diversity, Co-authored by 10 Authors – August 2018.
3. Leading: How to be your own boss! Co-authored by ten authors—September 2018.
4. Mau Mau Child Experience: Born and Raised in The Kenyan Mau Mau Uprising Era, The Autobiography of Alice Wanjikū Mangat—June 2018.
5. Profitable Teams, by Amina Chitembo—May 2018.
6. Pushing through Fear Stereotypes and Imperfect, by Amina Chitembo—December 2017.

7. The Serious Player's Decisive Business Start-up Guide, by Amina Chitembo—March 2017.

8. What Serious Executives and Business Owners Need to Know Before Hiring A High-Performance Coach, by Amina Chitembo.

You can learn more about our services at: https://www.diverse-cultures .co.uk/

Amina Chitembo

Amina Chitembo is a UK based British/ Zambian multi-award-winning Entrepreneur, Author, Speaker, Trainer, and Business High-Performance Coach. **She is the go-to coach for senior executives, leadership teams, and their staff.**

She consults, and trains integrated organisations and businesses, helping people to increase resilience, productivity, and profitability, while maintaining outstanding levels of high-performance and thereby improving mental health, wellbeing and financial stability in the workplace.

As an inspirational speaker, Amina champions **Leadership: The Link between Financial Stability and Mental Health in the Workplace.** She works internationally with leaders who juggle huge responsibilities of leading others, staying on top of business demands and profitability even in challenging times. After overcoming many difficulties to become a leader herself, she helps people to increase personal and professional success by challenging fears, stereotypes and defying imperfections, thereby reducing mental health issues.

NOTES

REVIEW REQUEST

Firstly, thanks a million for taking time to read my book. Your reviews are important to the authors and the publisher and as they say, there is no shame in asking for help.

If you enjoyed this book and learned something from it, you can help us in one or more of the following ways:

1. Go online, at www.amazon.co.uk or our website www .diverse-cultures.co.uk, write a kind review and give it a 5-star rating.
2. Buy the book as a gift for someone who could benefit from reading it.
3. Continue to grow and build the happy life and success you want.

Thank you.

An intriguing and captivating anthology from people you do not habitually associate with the term 'migrant'. The authors of the Perfect Migrant share experiences, twists, and turns of their journeys and their efforts to make a positive contribution. The book blasts the myth of the perfect migrant and highlights sheer strength and determination.

Written by; *Beatrice Hofmann, Charity Ngungi-Latz, Laura Tinzoh, Dr. Gianluca Zanini, Angelinah Boniface, Pamela Mahaka, Clara Meierdierks, Lucy Oyubo, Lwiza Mulenga, and Rod Khleif*

Diversity Series

www.diverse-cultures.co.uk

Printed in Poland
by Amazon Fulfillment
Poland Sp. z o.o., Wrocław

63363371R00134